W9-AUE-651

There is no substitute for a good reference book of strategies, definitions, and trading ideas like those found in this book. Every modern option trader using fast on-line fills and low commission rates - has to learn to rely on himself if he or she wishes to trade with the confidence it takes to make money consistently.

This publication is intended to provide training information and commentary on the subjects covered. It is sold with the understanding that neither the author nor the publisher is engaged in rendering legal, accounting, securities trading, or other professional services. If legal advice or other expert assistance is required, the services of a competent professional person should be sought.

Any stocks or trades, observations, and opinions based on real or fictitious equities, are used for illustration and teaching purposes only in this book- and are not intended to be trading advice on any specific equities or products.

About the Author

The author was a corporate trainer and commodity hedge manager for major corporations and brokerage companies for over 25 years. His articles have appeared on numerous blogs as well as *Futures Magazine, Stocks & Commodities Magazine*, plus other publications. His books emphasize the use of home & mobile device trading on powerful free, vendor-supplied software, and the use of deeply discounted commissions for individual investors.

The author's recent publication *Options Exposed Playbook – The Most Profitable and Popular Online Option Strategies of All Time* is becoming a popular standard for thousands of traders who value a straight-forward introduction to the methods and benefits of option trading. A simple and effective guide to hands-on investing, it is highly praised for its plain language and common sense approach to trading.

Those new to stock market investing might consider *Stock Market for Beginners Paycheck Freedom.* It is subtitled *The Easiest Guide to Personal Investing Ever Written* for good reason. It is both an introduction to stock investing and a collection of common-sense time-proven strategies from some of the most successful investors in history. Many parents provide this book to their children and grandchildren for motivation and to educate them on how to live a life without financial stress.

Any trader can take risk, a great trader can do it with purpose and use it to their advantage. – the author

The Amazing Covered Call
Triple Income Made Easy

BY DON A. SINGLETARY

Just because the market is open does not mean you have to trade. Cash is a position too.

Control your own destiny or someone else will.

Order your free BONUS chapter for this book now. Just send me an email to Don@WriteThisDown.com and put COVERED CALL in the subject line to receive the free PDF file. You get tips for dividend stock selection, an article on selecting stocks for covered calls, and other links to help you succeed.

Table of Contents

Introduction to a Cash Machine

What if you got a paycheck each and every month from your stock account for $500, $1000 or even $2000 per month? This book may well change the way you think about your trading account forever!

How would that change your life? What would you do knowing you had a consistent income coming in. I've been selling Covered-Calls for over 30 years. In the pages ahead, you'll read about Wally, a man who was sitting on a cash machine and did not know it. He had inherited thousands of shares of BellSouth when his beloved Mother passed. Wally kept those stock certificates in his safe at home and he received nice dividend check every three months but had no idea he was missing out of even more income. I, as a young broker in the 1980's, had the pleasure of introducing Wally to the covered-call strategy. He made an additional twenty-thousand dollars a year by simply by learning and using the strategy. You will also read about Carl, a man who retired from Georgia Power with over 43,000 shares of the parent company's (Southern Company) stock. I met Carl just a month ago, while having lunch at a local pub. I struck up a conversation with Carl, a total stranger. As you will read, Carl told me about his 41 years with his company and all the shares he owned and the dividends he now collects. I worked as a hedge consultant for 25 years. Carl was a very nice fellow and after chatting a while I asked him if he "wrote covered calls" on his stock. I could tell by the expression on his face, he knew nothing about them. Unfortunately for him, he wasn't interested in learning anything about them, so I dropped the subject. You will read about how much "free money" Carl is leaving on the table so-to-speak.

Two months ago, I got an email from a retired fellow who had read my *Options Exposed Playbook*. He explained to me that he owns stock in more than thirty-five companies, many of them Fortune 500 listings - and that he wants to know more about covered-calls. But he told me needed to learn more before he be comfortable using the strategy. Like many authors, I enjoy hearing from readers, and when I can, help them find strategies and information they need. This particular fellow by learning covered-calls, will increase his income by thousands of dollar per year and add virtually no additional risk to any of his holdings. I get asked about covered-calls more than any other subject.

Whether you are retired and own stock shares or if you are just starting out in personal investing, you need to know about using covered-calls. If you own stocks and don't know about them, it's like you have a cash machine in the basement and you just haven't turned it on yet.

I've been wanting to produce a book on this strategy for a long time and right after I met Carl, I wished I had already written this book, so I could have just given him a copy. You are going to read how he is leaving around $100,000 a year "on the table" by not selling covered calls. Just so you know, Carl isn't his real name (to protect his privacy). But I've got to tell you, if I ever see him again at the pub, I will give him a copy of this book and tell him, "Read this. You are "Carl"; please read this."

Using covered calls and cash-secured puts is so simple and so direct that these strategies are approved for use in self-directed tax deferred accounts like the IRA, 401k, and others. These strategies have nothing to do with the get-rich-quick and risky trades of "gunslinger" option traders. You are about to learn the kind of simple, tried-and-true trading that hundreds of thousands of professional money managers use every day.

"If you can't explain it simply, you don't understand it well enough." –Albert Einstein

I promise you plain language and common sense in the pages ahead. There is no need to expound on theories and mathematical models for you to be able to employ these three simple trading methods. They won't just make a difference in your retirement; these simple lessons will make you a more valuable and smarter trader for the rest of your life. Learn them; teach them to your children and to your friends when possible – and they will be forever grateful. The triple income refers to the following strategies in this book:

- Covered Calls
- Cash-Secured Puts
- Dividend Reinvestment Plans

It is very important that you understand, that using the covered-call strategy does not mean you have to sell your shares of stock. Most times, the strategy is used to sell options (and collecting money), and the options expire worthless. You will learn to manage the strategy as you gain experience using covered-calls. The first example in the next chapter will use an illustration that does sell the underlying stock, but that is so you will learn the mechanics and definitions of the strategy. It is possible to be "called away" have to sell your shares, but it is avoidable except in rare circumstances.

Very Important: Remember, with stock options, each option is for 100 shares of stock.

Chapter 1 Mechanics: How the Covered Call Works

The covered call is considered to be among the most simple of stock option strategies. They present a way for owners of stocks to capture additional income. In a manner of speaking, people will actually pay you to sell your stock at a profit. Each option represents 100 share of stock.

Here's an example: If you own a hundred shares of stock at a price of $40.00, and that is currently trading at $48 a share, there are traders who will buy stock options to purchase your stock at $50. They might, for example pay you $2.50 per share for the right to purchase your stock anytime in the next 30 days at $50.00 per share. For 100 shares at $2.50 per share, that's a total of $250. The purchaser of this $50-strike CALL option is willing to gamble that your stock's price will increase to over $50 during a time interval, in this example over the next 30 days. If the buyer of this CALL option is wrong, he will lose the entire $250. If the buyer (aka: purchaser) of this CALL is correct, he stands to make a profit based on how much your stock goes over the price of $52.50, the strike price of $50 + the $2.50 per share he or she paid for the option.

If your stock is over $50 at the expiration date in thirty days, your stock is sold for $50 as it is "called away" from you. You bought the stock at $40, so you make ten dollars per share (the strike minus the purchase price, or $50 minus $40. And you also get paid the options price (called the "premium") of $2.50 per share, a total of 100 shares times $2.50 = $250. So your total profit is = 100 shares X $10 per share, plus $250 = $1250.

If, on the expiration date of the option, your stock is $50 or less, the option "expires worthless" and you get to keep the premium ($250) you collected at the time you sold the option.

Let's go over the terms used here to describe this transaction:

The PURCHASE PRICE of your stock was $40.
The TRADE PRICE at the time you sold the option was $48.

The PRICE OF THE OPTION, also known as THE PREMIUM was quoted as $2.50, which means $250 because the option is for 100 shares @ $2.50 each.

The STRIKE PRICE of the option is $50.00

The STRIKE PRICE of $50 described to be OUT-OF-THE-MONEY (stated as OTM) because the price of your stock at the time of the transaction is BELOW the STRIKE PRICE of the CALL option.

Here is a description of all possible outcomes for you:

IF AT EXPIRATION, in thirty days:

1) Your stock's price was under $50, you keep the $250. The buyer of the CALL options loses the $250 she paid for the option and you still own your stock.

2) Your stock's price was over $50: Your stock is CALLED AWAY at the STRIKE PRICE of $50. You no longer own the stock, it was sold for $50 (the funds are deposited into your account) and you made a $10 per share profit, plus another $2.50 per share (100 shares = $250).

3) Your stock's price went down: The CALL option expires worthless, but you keep the $250 PREMIUM you received for selling (aka: writing) the CALL option. You still own the stock of course at whatever it's current TRADING PRICE happens to be.

In all of these outcomes, you still keep the $2.50 per share (total: $250) you received at the time you sold (aka: wrote) the COVERED CALL.

What you gave up, when you SOLD (wrote) the COVERED CALL was ANY GAINS YOU MIGHT HAVE MADE IF YOUR STOCK WAS TRADING FOR OVER $52.50 per share.

For example: If your stock at expiration was trading at $53.25, you NET OUT at (50 + 2.5) $52.50 per share, and you did not make the money exceeding that price. You DID NOT PROFIT any gains over $52.50 per share. In this case, that amount is (53.25 minus 52.50) or $.75 per share ($75.)

Here is a chart that depicts this transaction of selling the covered call for XYZ stocks at a STRIKE of 50 ($50):

An investor who owns stock (or who will buy it) can write (sell) options on an equivalent amount of stock and collect the premium income *without adding additional risk.*

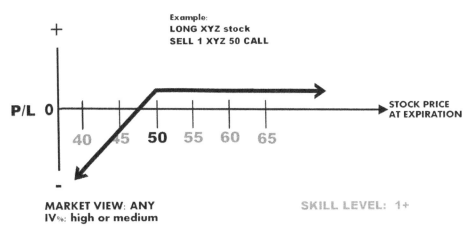

COVERED CALL

Example:
LONG XYZ stock
SELL 1 XYZ 50 CALL

P/L 0

STOCK PRICE AT EXPIRATION

40   45   **50**   55   60   65

MARKET VIEW: ANY
IV%: high or medium

SKILL LEVEL: 1+

MAXIMUM GAIN: Strike price - Stock purchase price + premium of CALL
MAXIMUM LOSS: Stock purchase price - premium received

If you own a stock (or buy it), you can sell a covered CALL option with a strike higher than the stock price (an OTM CALL) and the *premium* is *credited* to your account. If at option expiration, the stock is below the strike, the CALL expires worthless and you keep the credit. If the stock is at or above the strike of the CALL option at expiration, you are obligated to sell the stock at the strike price. What you risk is any gains you might have made from the sale of the stock *above* the strike price (aka: opportunity cost).

COVERED CALL example:

Scenario: You own 100 shares of XYZ that you bought at $40/share six months ago. Suppose that stock is now trading at $48. You might be able to sell a 50-strike CALL that expires in 30 days for a premium of 2.50.

If you hold both the stock and the short CALL until expiration AND the stock is trading at $50 or above – the stock will be 'called away' (the CALL option is exercised) at the $50 strike price. When you sold the CALL, you became *obligated* to sell the stock at the strike price of $50, *if the option is exercised*. The net result is that you profited from the stock gains and you collected the premium of the CALL. 2.50 + 50 less cost of of the stock at $40 = net profit of $1250, $250 more than if you had just held the stock to sell at $50/share; that's an 'extra' 25% (250/1000).

If you hold both the stock and the short CALL until expiration AND the stock is trading *below* the 50 strike at expiration, you collect the $250 premium and you still own the stock at whatever price it is trading at that day.

Very few options are exercised unless they are ITM (IN-THE-MONEY) at expiration, but you should understand that a CALL option can be exercise *at any time during the contract* (through the expiration date). If this happens, you keep the option CALL premium credited to your account and you are obligated to sell the stock at $50. When the CALL option is exercised, your broker will deliver your shares and put the credit into your account; this is done automatically (by your broker.)

An investor owning a stock doesn't have to sell an at-the-money (ATM) call. Choosing a strike price simply involves a tradeoff between priorities. You sell a higher strike if you are very bullish on the stock and you would be willing to sell at the STRIKE PRICE (because you will have the obligation to do that if the options expires while IN-THE-MONEY (ITM).

The covered call writer could select a higher, further out-of-the-money strike price and preserve more of the stock's upside potential for the duration of the strategy. However, the further out-of-the-money call would generate less premium income, which means there would be a smaller downside cushion in case of a stock decline. But whatever the choice, the strike price (plus the premium) should represent an acceptable liquidation price.

Consider timing: If you own a stock and are expecting a price rise soon, you could regret losing the stock during a price rally; this is a consideration before selling a covered call. If you write a covered call and the price rises unexpectedly and you wish to hold on to the stock, the only way out is to buy back the CALL – and this would likely cost you; at least some of the loss would be covered by the call premium you collected and the increased price of the stock.

The great thing about writing (selling) a covered call is that the investor can choose the strike price; normally a strike price OTM (above the stock's current price) is sold. As more distant (higher) strikes are sold, the amount of premium you collect will decrease.

Another potentially very important consideration is the tax you might have to pay. If you have a large profit in stock you are holding, then you could owe substantial taxes if it is 'called away' (the short call is exercised). You should seek tax advice if you are at all in doubt of what you might owe. This is assuming you are not writing covered calls in a tax-deferred account. Since there are no tax consequences in a tax-deferred account, the covered-CALL strategy is ideal in this type of account.

Selling Covered Calls in Tax Deferred Accounts Can Be One of the Best Strategies

Most self-directed tax deferred accounts are allowed to use the COVERED CALL strategy; not all brokerages, trading companies, or custodians allow it. You have the right to move your account in most cases or to ask to change the restrictions. Of course whether you should or not - is not within the scope of this book. Having said that, selling covered calls in tax deferred accounts is quite common and done all the time. Just so you know, trading your stocks and covered calls in your tax-deferred account is "in a self-directed account." This is the specific language to describe a tax-deferred account where you do all your own investing.

Selling covered CALLS in tax-deferred accounts is one of the safest and most dependable ways to increase an investors return from 5%, 10%, or more annually. Many investors have stocks in these accounts that pay dividends, and also the stock's price rises over time. Selling covered calls on these and other stocks can simply add another source of income.

Weekly and Monthly Options

Here's how to read the option listings on a stock. This example is using TD Ameritrade's Think or Swim trading platform; others are very similar to this standard type listing.

This example is for Ford options. The "Last X" means last trade and $11.25 per share is the price.

The OPTION CHAIN lists the options available for Ford. Options are named for their EXPIRATION DATES. For example, the " >26 MAY 17" means the options listed here expire 26th of MAY 2017. The "(45)" is the number of days until the option expires. The "100" means they are for 100 shares of the underlying stock, Ford in this case.

The MONTHLY options are all listed without the designation (Weeklys) after the row. Option listing are arranged from the nearby dates out to the more distant dates. The "Weeklys" are only available for a month to six weeks out; this is normal.

All options expire on a Friday. All the Monthly options expire the 3rd Friday of the named Month.

By clicking on the ">" by each named option, you get a drop down box of all the options STRIKES available for that CLASS of the options. This table that has the options bid/ ask price, STRIKES available, the open interest, and other parameters is called the option MATRIX.

For example, here is the MATRIX for "> 26 MAY 17": Remember that F is trading at: $11.23 per share:

			CALLS			Strikes: 8						PUTS	
Net Chng	Prob.OT...	Last X		Bid X	Ask X	Exp	Strike	Bid X	Ask X	Net Chng	Prob.OT...		Last X
⌄ 19 MAY 17	(38)	100											30.45%
0	12.80%	0		3.15 M	3.45 M	19 MAY 17	8	0 J	.01 Z	0	98.70%		.04 X
-.06	0.00%	2.19 A		2.19 X	2.26 I	19 MAY 17	9	.02 Z	.03 Z	0	94.66%		.03 M
-.04	9.25%	1.26 C		1.19 X	1.29 X	19 MAY 17	10	.08 Z	.09 Z	0	84.04%		.08 E
-.01	42.97%	.43 X		.43 Z	.44 H	19 MAY 17	11	.32 X	.33 Q	0	55.14%		.32 X
-.01	83.23%	.09 Q		.08 Z	.09 H	19 MAY 17	12	.99 Z	1.00 X	+.04	23.10%		1.00 I
0	96.61%	.02 C		.01 Z	.02 Z	19 MAY 17	13	1.87 T	1.99 T	+.03	12.04%		1.93 I
0	98.95%	.01 X		0 J	.01 Z	19 MAY 17	14	2.87 C	2.98 M	0	8.73%		2.41 Z
0	99.26%	.01 X		0 J	.01 Z	19 MAY 17	15	3.75 M	4.00 M	0	4.70%		3.89 C

⌄ Option Chain   Filter: Off   Spread: Single   Layout: Net Change, Probability OTM, Last X

The "19 MAY 17" expire on May 19, 2017 in (38) days. Notice the CALLS are on the left side of the matrix and the PUTS on the right side. The STRIKES are in the middle and this selection is from $8.00 to $15.00.
Note the bid/ask prices of each option.

Question: What is the bid/ask price of the 19MAY17, 12-STRIKE CALL?
Answer: bid/ask is: .08/.09

Question: What was the last trade price of that option? **Answer:** .09

Question: What is the Prob OTM of this option?
Answer: The second column is "Prob OTM" or "Probability this option will expire Out of The Money (OTM) is 83.23%. Based on math alone, not the stocks fundamentals, that is the chance it will expire worthless (and if you sold it, you keep that money.)

Question: If you owned 1000 shares of Ford, and sold ten of these CALLS, how much premium do you get credited to your account?

Answer: If you sold at .08, you get $8.00 times 10 options = $80, and you have an 83.23% chance of keeping that money and your stock. (This example ignores the small commission to keep things simple for now.)

This sale of the ten covered calls will gain you a credit of $80. The options expire in 38 days. The value of 1,000 shares of Ford (F), is $11,230. $80/$11230 = a return of .71% When this is annualized (365/38 = 9.6. So 9.6 times .71% = an annualize return of 6.8%.

Ford pays (at the time this is written of course) a dividend return of 5.34%. By continually writing (selling) covered call options year round, the total return, not including gains if any from the stock, would be about 6.8% + 5.34% = 12.14% annually. This did not include the cost of commissions in selling the calls, so the return would actually be a slightly less.

An Example Using KO stock (Coca Cola)

Note: This example was a few years ago, but still displays the strong characteristics of the strategy that remain today.

Selling Covered Calls can make money even when a stock price:
Goes up, Remains the Same, or Goes Down

The investor usually selects a call option strike OTM (Out-of-The-Money), above the stock price) to sell. If you are selling calls (also called *writing calls*) on a stock that you have in the 'long term hold' category (meaning you are not thinking of selling it at this time and are holding it for (more) long term gains, you may simply sell a CALL far OTM, and collect the premium. In the case of such stocks, the investor who has owned it for some time – has likely been paying attention. The investor is familiar with potential earnings, earnings reports, trading ranges, price volatility of the stock, and in many cases - the investor follows news on the stock for months and often years. In other words, if you were a hunter, you could say you "know this animal and his habits very well." If the investor has stocks like this, or even if he doesn't own it yet and is very familiar with it's price behavior – then that stock could be a good candidate for the covered call strategy – also sometimes called *the covered write*. Understanding a stock's range of trading is key to choosing covered call strategies. If the investor can select a call strike to sell that the stock is not likely to reach over the short term – and think the premium of selling the call is worth the additional risk, then this investor will likely keep the premium in all these three cases: 1) the stock goes up, but not above the strike, 2) the stock price remains the same, or 3) the stock price goes down and the investor doesn't mind continuing to hold the stock (aka: "staying long.")

Review Point: There is a very important parameter in your trading software to help you make decisions; it is 'Prob OTM.' This can be shown in your trading matrix for a stock's options and it literally means "the probability this option strike will be out-of-the-money on the date the option expires."

The example used is here is only for illustration; by the time you read this all the parameters will have changed and the options expired. We'll use the KO option matrix for CALLS. We use this *matrix* to examine possible strikes to sell using the 'Prob OTM' parameter. We'll examine the option premiums for various strikes, and then we'll discuss some choices. The objective of this example is to take the reader through a typical scenario and to discuss some considerations when selecting a call option to sell.

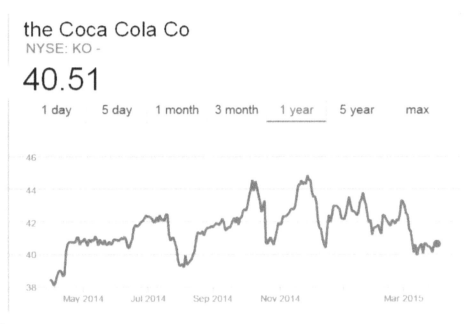

the Coca Cola Co
NYSE: KO -

40.51

| 1 day | 5 day | 1 month | 3 month | 1 year | 5 year | max |

For this example, remember this stock is currently priced at 40.51 per share, the JUN 15 options are 80 days until expiration, and the AUG 15 class expires in 143 days. Notice in the one-year chart KO is 40.51 and has traded near 45 twice in the last twelve months and is currently only about 3.5 dollars from its low of the last year near 38. KO is the type of blue-chip stock that many retirement portfolios choose to buy-and-hold. From a technical standpoint there seems to be price resistance near 45 and significant price support just above 40. KO has been trading in a defined range for at least the last six months. None of this takes away from the view that KO is a good long-term buy-and-hold investment.

It isn't always the thing to do - but in this example, we'll choose to sell a call from the JUN 2015 class; the reasoning being that there seems to be more certainty about price behavior in the next 80 days, than in the longer AUG 15's 143 days until option expiration.

This is a good time to point out the difference in the 45 call options prices between KO **JUN** 45 CALL, priced at .15 ($15 each) and the more distant KO **AUG** 45 CALL priced at .35 ($35 each).

Now you are ready to hear about a perfectly boring trade that will make you money and generate income on a regular basis. As you view the matrix, you could be thinking that because of KO price behavior of the past year, the KO stock probably won't trade above a price of 45 within the next 80 days. Look at the price of the KO JUN 45 CALL and you will see the market agrees with you; the price is bid/ask

Stock:	Coca Cola	Symbol KO	Price 40.51			
CALLS	Class JUN 15	Days until Exp 80				
Strike:	Bid	Ask	Last	Delta	IV%	Prob OTM
36	4.70	4.80	4.70	0.85	17.88%	19.87%
37	3.80	3.90	3.85	0.8	17.57%	24.60%
38	2.95	3.05	3.00	0.74	17.41%	30.92%
39	2.19	2.24	2.20	0.65	17.61%	39.06%
40	1.54	1.59	1.55	0.55	18.19%	49.34%
41	1.03	1.06	1.04	0.43	19.02%	60.52%
42	0.65	0.67	0.66	0.32	20.13%	71.34%
43	0.39	0.42	0.41	0.22	21.94%	80.40%
44	0.24	0.26	0.25	0.15	23.84%	87.01%
45	0.14	0.17	0.15	0.10	25.94%	91.55%

CALLS	Class AUG 15	Days until Exp 143				
Strike:	Bid	Ask	Last	Delta	IV%	Prob OTM
36	4.80	4.95	4.85	0.81	17.69%	25.66%
37	3.95	4.10	4.00	0.76	17.68%	30.71%
38	3.20	3.30	3.25	0.69	17.00%	37.01%
39	2.48	2.66	2.52	0.62	17.74%	44.13%
40	1.89	1.95	1.92	0.53	18.16%	52.25%
41	1.38	1.44	1.40	0.44	18.81%	60.67%
42	0.99	1.03	1.01	0.35	19.53%	68.82%
43	0.70	0.75	0.72	0.28	20.72%	75.93%
44	0.49	0.51	0.50	0.21	21.78%	82.10%
45	0.34	0.37	0.35	0.16	23.16%	86.72%

0.14/0.17 and the last trade is at .15. Also you read in the Prob OTM column that there is (at least) mathematically a 91.55% chance the option will expire worthless (meaning you keep the premium and your KO stock will not likely be called away (or be ITM, In-The-Money). Now you must determine the true viability of the trade: Will it make enough money considering the low risk of the trade? Of course, each one of us has different risk adversity, investment philosophy, and risk tolerance. Now, let's do the numbers on this trade. Let's say we intend to consider selling ten of the KO JUN 45 CALLS at a price of $15 (.15) each for a total of $150.00 credit from the options premium.

Of course we must consider a number of things. How much commission will we have to pay to sell ten of these options? Commonly, online accounts are charging from 65 cents to $2.00 per option. Obviously, if you use a full service broker (*financial representative* they are often called), it might cost you $10 or more per option – and there's no way you can pay $10 each to trade a $15 option – 2/3 of your credit would go to paying the commissions and your risk versus reward is skewed past common sense and good money management. (Please remember this book is for low commission online investors using free vendor provided software. This doesn't ignore or discount the value of a good broker/consultant and $10 is a perfectly reasonable commission for trades handled in person by a live broker instead of trading electronically.) I am pointing out that you can place trades with very low commissions, that are just not practical when paying $10 or more per side or 'each way'. (each way means 'in' and 'out' of the trade).

In our example, I will use not the lowest or highest commission rates of online trading, but will use something in between that usually doesn't require a huge deposit or minimum number of trades to maintain. The commission rate used in this example is $1.50 per option on each side of a trade (you pay $1.50 to buy and/or sell it 'each way').

Selling 10 of the KO JUN 45 CALLS will gain us a credit of $150, minus (10 x $1.50) a $15 commission, a net credit in our account of $135. Remember, since you own the stock you are not required to put up any margin (deposit) to make the trade; you are selling *covered calls*, meaning the stock is the collateral for the trade. For these ten options, the underlying is 1,000 shares of KO.

So how do we know this trade is worth it? I know plenty of investors that wouldn't give any consideration to a trade that only has a maximum $135 upside. One could sell ten of the 43-strikes for .40 and collect $400 - $15 commission for a net credit of $385, and the trade would have a 75.33% chance of total success. I am using the more conservative example choice here and I'll tell you why. Many, certainly not all, of the readers of this book are new to option trading; they want to tread carefully until they are more comfortable with all the new terms and have more experience trading with the software their vendor has provided. If you are already confident and your goals and risk adversity can tolerate more risk, that is your choice. I have learned from teaching and talking with new option investors that most of them prefer to take things slowly until they build up more experience and confidence. I don't judge; that's not my job – but it is my advice to neophyte option traders to take things slowly until your confidence builds. Make some lower risk trades, follow along, get used to the terms and software. Even many experienced traders might be new to low-commission online trading methods. Most traders will be successful at learning their own limits and abilities over time; I urge you to trust that.

The example of selling those ten KO JUN 45 CALLS is the **covered call** strategy – and does require you either own or buy the underlying shares; since each option represents 100 shares, it takes 10 x 100 = 1,000 shares of KO in your account – and trading at $40.51 per share they are worth $40, 510. In no way is it realistic to expect most new option traders to have that kind of resources for only one trade (although a great many do). For this reason, I'll include a second example here; an example that dollar-wise is not a large risk, but it won't require a large amount of capital either.

Let's assume you own 100 shares of KO, worth $4,051. Go back to the KO JUN 15 matrix and consider selling one of the KO JUN 43 CALLS for .40 or $40. After the $1.50 commission, you net $38.50 and you still have the Prob OTM of 80.40%, pretty nice odds. If you tell a friend you are learning to trade options and just 'made $38.50' by clicking your mouse or tapping the screen two times - they might not get very excited. After all $38.50 isn't much money. Remember, the purpose of these types of trades, would be what I call 'training-wheels' trades; use them to learn, gain confidence, get experience. Learn to trade smart and understand all you can about the risks of option trading. My way of looking at it is not that "I only made $38.50 for clicking a mouse a few times" but to think of it as "getting paid to go to school." I happened to have used KO in this example, but you might consider the strategy using a stock you already own of course.

I promise it will be worth it in the end for you to put in the time and effort to gain the knowledge and experience. Many options traders, a great many actually, do jump in over their heads - and when they lose money doing it, I assure you they rarely tell everybody about the mistakes they make. Far more than half the people working in this country don't make $38.50 an hour and you already know how to make that much in only five minutes! That's a rate of $462 an hour. I would say that is a good rate to be paid 'while you are learning'.

Trading these low-commission, small transactions online is an ideal way to learn; the dollar amounts are relatively small. The type of trade just described is pretty low-risk, and you can do small trades like this with several different stocks at once, then track them all and learn! And you get to do it all privately in your online account; this privacy is actually very liberating and allows you to learn faster.

There are great rewards for learning the skills, math, theory, investment methods, strategies, and even the patience it takes to be a good trader of options. Yes, patience is a valuable commodity; not everybody has it or can get it. Patience is like experience, you learn it over time - you will be paid very, very well for learning it.

GAIN THE KNOWLEDGE   DO THE WORK   TRADE SMART   MAKE THE MONEY

Another Great Advantage of Selling Covered CALLS

About 75 to 80% of all options expire worthless. This means the odds of you making money *selling* them is much greater than *buying* them. Provided you are writing covered CALLs on your long-term buy and hold stocks, there is very little *additional* risk when you sell CALLs on these stock that you own (or have chosen to buy.) Provided you are selling CALLs only on your long-term stocks, selling these covered calls is among the most conservative and relatively safe option strategies. It has an inherent advantage to all investors learning to trade options: Trading covered calls has almost all the components you need to learn about trading options. You will learn option pricing, how to use your vendor software to study individual option parameters, you'll become familiar with terms, you learn about time-decay, how to compare option prices and classes, about using Prob of OTM and Prob of ITM computations, and you get to do all this while not exposing yourself past your risk tolerance.

How to Reduce Your Cost Basis in Stocks by Continuously Selling Covered Calls

As you sell covered calls, if you choose wisely - you will profit more often than not. As you gain experience with selling those calls you also will continue to learn more about specific underlying stocks and their price patterns and trading ranges.

When you sell covered calls on underlying stocks that you own (or buy), as they expire and you collect credits from the premium, it will definitely occur to you to keep doing it. Many times after you've sold one covered call and it becomes relatively worthless (a good thing as you have sold it, not bought it), you will have little to gain by waiting for the little amount of premium left to decay completely, so you can buy it back – for much less than you sold it for – keep the profit, then sell another option farther out in time. This process of closing one position and simultaneously selling another option is called *rolling out.* As you continue to roll out, this strategy will continually reduce your cost basis in the stock. Over long periods of time, these profits can add up – and it might only take you a few minutes each week or month to maintain these trades – and all the while you are continually making money.

Another example of rolling out short calls is when the underlying stock rises above the strike you sold - and to keep from being assigned (you are obligated to sell the stock), you need to close the position. As you do this, buy back the calls you sold (at a loss) by 'rolling out'. You may choose to roll out; that is to cover the ITM short call, and simultaneously sell a call *farther out* in time and with a *higher strike that is OTM*. This way you get to keep the stock, and although you might lose money initially as you roll out your short call position, you can continue to sell covered calls over time to increase your net profits.

Here's an example of rolling out:

You wrote a covered call on XYZ stock when the stock price was $47.50. You sold a nearby OTM 55 call option, and before the option expires the stock goes up to $57.25. You have made significant gains in the rising stock value for sure; more than enough to offset the loss of having to buy the 55 call back to close the position at a higher price than you sold it for (a loss). You may go out another three months or six months in time and sell a higher strike, a

THE AMAZING COVERED CALL

65 for example and collect the premium. This is *rolling out the position*; in this case it might be called *rolling up* to a higher strike, and *out* to a more distant month.

The stock gains have been much more than the loss when you bought the 55 call back to close your trade – and you continue to write covered calls on the underlying stock you own. Buying the 55 call back (to close the position) insured you would not be assigned at the options expiration. ('being assigned in this case with a short call would mean you would have had to sell the stock at the strike of 55.) What you have lost is most of the gains your stock made above the strike price (55). This is because you had to buy back the 55 strike for more than you sold it for to keep from selling the underlying stock.

No matter how good you are at trading options and stocks, remember nobody has 100% winners. Part of keeping your momentum going is to realize this. Don't let having a few losing trades bother you; competitive people often have problems accepting any losses but they are a part of the process.

There is a saying among poker players, "Scared money never wins." If you are trading and always preoccupied with potential losses, you are likely trading out of your risk tolerance and/or your resources limits. If you have the resources and time to trade and do not enjoy it or find it too stressful - you must either quit trading, find a lower risk which you can tolerate, or consider finding someone who can help you with your investments. Everybody loves to make money trading, but not everybody has the risk tolerance or the resources to avoid 'trading scared'. It's only human that when people are outside the limits of their risk tolerance, fear keeps them from making rational decisions. Remember, it is not rational to expect 100% winners even though it is logical to strive for that.

Questions & Answers Chapter Review

Question: I think I understand how to write (sell) covered CALLs, but I'm still not comfortable with the idea. What else can I do to learn more?

Answer: First of all, relax; that's the way almost everybody feels when they start out with this strategy. The advice in this book is geared to people who trade their own account(s) online. Using an online broker almost always means you are paying low commissions. So what ARE "low commissions?" For buying and selling stock, online brokers charge a set fee; this means whether you are buying or selling 10 shares or 10,000 shares, the cost for the transaction will be the same. This fee is usually from $4.95 to $9.95. The fees for trading your options should be from $.75 per option to about $2.00 per option. You will have to phone and talk to your online broker and they can adjust the published rate to give you a better rate in some cases. For example: They will likely ask you how many options per month on the average you will be trading. If you can answer 50 to 100 or more, you should get the lower rate. On the other hand, if you let them know you are starting out and will only be trading 10 or less per month, you will probably have to pay something around $2.00 per option. There is a small section in this book about how to open an account, if you need that information. It is a simple process, and only takes five minutes. Now, about learning more about using covered CALLs: Your online broker (any of them) will have an "education" listing at their web site. You can go to that section and search for "covered calls" and you should be able to find several professionally produced free videos to watch. There is also some written information you can review to go with that. If you have trouble finding these things, just phone them and ask; they are glad to help you. Be sure to email me for your free BONUS to get some link that can also help. Don@WriteThisDown.com and COVERED CALLS in the subject line please.

Another great way to learn is to use your broker's "paper trading" software feature. This allows you to practice with "paper money" so you can learn to use the trading software. Many brokers will allow a person to use a free trial version, so you can see if you favor their platform for trading. Don't be shy about phoning and telling them you are shopping for a broker and want to try out their *trading platform*, which is what they call their software. If you are new at option trading be sure to tell them you will be trading covered calls and buying and selling stocks. Many brokers have more than one version of their trading program; letting them know what you will need helps them direct you to the appropriate version. Remember, everyone who trades options was new at one time and needed this introductory help. Ask for videos and help when you need it. The reason I recommend you use the video from your broker is simple really. The brokers (all of them) have professionally produced help videos. Although, there are scores of videos on places like YouTube, many of them are poor quality and/or someone is "trying to sell you something" and may not give your pure information and instruction. It can be confusing if you are a beginner, so make sure you view the "good stuff."

Question: How do I know WHICH call option to sell?
Answer: The short answer is this: Pick an option that with an expiration date of 30 to 60 days out. Then, pick a STRIKE about 5% or more above your stock's current trading price. Some will tell you to try and sell a CALL that is about 1% of the price of your stock. As you gain experience, you will be more comfortable. The reason there is no straight mathematical formula for selecting a CALL to sell, if that it is as much art and feel, as it is math. As times goes by and you gain experience, you will know what the normal trading range of your stock is for a day, week, month, or even annually; you "get to know" the typical price behavior of your stock. And keep in mind, your online broker will have "paper trading" features in the software so you can practice without risking real money until you gain an amount of comfort. And in case you are wondering, "no," paper-trading is NOT the same as real money – but it's as close as you can get to the real thing. I'll add a training note here: Using the "paper money" mode helps a lot. Once you have actually tried it and you still have a problem and need help, it's a LOT easier to phone and get help when you have tried the product. This allows you to learn faster actually.

Question: What if a bull market has my stock on meteoric rise, do I still sell covered CALLs?
Answer: The short answer is "no." Unfortunately, a vast majority of the time in the stock market, is not a runaway "bull market." You may have some stocks in your portfolio that are not the best selections to be selling covered CALLs on. If you have a relatively small company's stock that you bought for speculation, it might not be suitable at all. Please keep in mind, the best stocks for covered CALL writing (selling) are usually large cap (big companies) stocks that trade millions of shares a day, not small new companies or speculative investments. If your stock is seeming to rise fast in a bull market, you should consider either selling CALLs with a higher-strike, or perhaps just letting your profits run up on the stock and not sell options on it for a while. What if the market (and your stock's value) is going down in "bear" mode? Then, you may want to consider selling At-The-Money

(ATM) or In-The-Money (ITM) CALL options. The premium you collect will be higher than usual and can help offset the losses on your stock.

Question: What if my stock is close to a price at which I want to sell my shares?

Answer: To answer this, I'll use an example. Suppose you own 500 shares of XYZ stock and it is currently trading at 78.80 dollars a share and you would be glad to sell it at or near 80 per share? You can opt to sell either: a) an ITM (In-The-Money) 75 CALL for 5.00 or more, or b) you can sell an 80 CALL. In selling the 80-strike CALL, you can essentially "get paid" to do what you want to do anyway (which is selling the stock at 80 or higher.) If you do sell the 80 CALL and it is not exercised, you can go out another month and sell another 80-strike again and again, until your stock is sold. All the while, you "get paid" for waiting to sell it at your target price. Of course, deciding to "hold" the stock longer means you are subject to losses if the stock declines in price.

Review of This Chapter

A CALL option is a contract on 100 shares of stock.

The SELLER of the CALL agrees to deliver 100 shares of the stock if the CALL is exercised. Technically, the options can be exercised at any time until it expires.

Though the option may be exercised at ANY time before or on the expiration date of the option, it is not usually exercised unless it is ATM or ITM (at-the-money or in-the-money). This means the stock's price is at or above the STRIKE PRICE of the option.

The SELLER of the option has an OBLIGATION. The BUYER of the option has a RIGHT.

If the CALL is exercised, the SELLER must deliver 100 shares of the stock. When you own the stock, this is done by your broker automatically; the proceeds from the stock (the money they are worth at the STRIKE-PRICE) is credited to your account. You do NOT need to do anything for this to happen; it is automatic because this is what you have agreed to do. When the option was sold, you are credited the option's price (the "premium") at the time you sold the option. So the total credit to your account is the stock sale proceeds and the PREMIUM you received for the option.

After the CALL option(s) is exercised, you are free to buy the stock again, and you may choose sell another CALL option on it at any time.

What you risk losing as a result of selling the CALL(s), is the gain on stock (if any) that is ABOVE the STRIKE PRICE. And of course, if your stock goes down instead of up, you will lose some of the value of the stock (but in this case your sold CALL will NOT be exercised but just expire worthless – and then you may write (sell) option(s) again.

You never want to SELL more CALLS than you can "cover". For example if you own 400 shares of a stock, you can sell as many as 4 CALLs that are covered. Selling more than you can cover, will result in theoretically unlimited risks. A CALL that is not "covered" is called a NAKED CALL; and these have theoretically unlimited risks.

What a Difference An Additional Yield Can Make

It is common to use covered calls to increase your investment yields by 5 to 15% a year. Here is an example of how powerful a seemingly small 5% boost can be in your investments.

**If you start with $5,000 and add $200 per Month,
this is how long it takes to have $1,000,000:**

Yield	Time	Goal
5%	59.81 Years	$1,000,000
8%	42.42 Years	$1,000,000
10%	35.79 Years	$1,000,000
15%	26.02 Years	$1,000,000
18%	22.46 Years	$1,000,000

Just a few percentage points can reduce your time until financial independence by a third to a half!

Right now your bank's certificates of deposit yield less than 5%. Unless you are a real estate wizard or have your own very profitable business, the stock market is the most accessible way for a person to expect reasonable life-long returns. The S&P in the last 25-years has yielded about 9.8%. If you would like to run some scenarios for yourself, there is a free "When will you be a millionaire?" calculator on the web at: https://dqydj.com/when-will-you-be-a-millionaire/ I suggest you try a few of your own scenarios there; you will how extremely important it is to have extra yield strategies (like covered calls).

Be sure to send me an email to: Don@WriteThisDown.com with "Covered Calls" in the subject line, so I can send you a free BONUS chapter that has many such links and other material to help you plan your investments. It's FREE, and no registration of any kind is required, so why not do it now?

Chapter 2: The Amazing Covered Call

Not very often, but just once in a rare while do we experienced "free money" or "found money." Like when you find an extra $20 or fifty-dollar-bill in your pants pocket or in some drawer, purse, or wallet that you missed or had completely forgotten. I want to share a "found money" story with you from over 35 years ago. It wasn't I who found money, it was a friend and client of mine named Wally. While a stock broker in the 1980's, I met Wally, the owner of a small chain of clothing stores. Wally was a hard-working middle-aged man, divorced, a great business man, and I was lucky to have him as a good client. After knowing him about six months, we were in my office talking and he mentioned to me that he had 38,000 shares of BellSouth he'd inherited from his Mother's family. He said he had the share certificates at home in his safe and that for sentimental reasons, he had never considered selling or trading the shares; he was more than well-enough off financially not to need the money.

The first thing I thought of is how much money Wally could be making if he would sell covered-calls on some of those 38,000 shares of BellSouth, so I suggested to Wally he put the shares on deposit in his account so we could start making money selling CALLs against the stock. Wally balked, big time. I had assumed since he was a savvy business man, he knew about the COVERED CALL strategy. Wrong! All he knew was that "options are risky" and that he wanted nothing to do with them; this is a common misconception even now. It's just human nature that makes people afraid of things they do not understand; it's a fact of life. But this story has a happy ending.

Wally had mentioned to me that he and his girlfriend were leaving for the Bahamas in a few days, so I asked him (remember this is the mid-1980's), "How much will your entire weekend in the Bahamas cost, including flights, meals, drinks, and incidentals?" He looked at me weird, and then said, "About $2,000."

I knew two things about Wally: He like to enjoy himself, and he absolutely loved to save money and was always looking for a bargain. So I looked up the price of CALL options for

BellSouth, and computed how many CALL options he could sell, to get a $2500 deposit into his account the next morning. I told him, all you have to do is to bring your share certificates into the office and let us hold them for you, then I can sell covered calls on a few thousand shares and deposit the $2500 into your account the next day. As I said, Wally was a good business man, so his reply was, "Can you give me the money in cash this Friday morning at 10AM?" This was four days away and would be easy to do, so I answered, "Consider it done!" He sent somebody over that afternoon to bring in his share certificates and they were credited to his account the next morning. I wrote the CALL options and collected just over $2,500, which was deposited to Wally's account. I then instructed the cashier at our office to have the $2500 in cash ready for Wally when he showed up Friday morning.

Wally showed up alright, with his girlfriend on his arm, flip-flops on, and he was already dressed in a loud-colored tourist shirt ready for the beach. He didn't even sit down, he just put out his hand and said, "Where's my cash?" I took him to the cashier's window and they counted out twenty-five crisp, new 100 dollar bills for him. He said, "That was easy," and immediately asked, "How much more can we make selling those covered calls?"

I answered, "You get to the airport and have a great weekend. We can talk when you get back next week, and there's plenty more where that came from." Wally not only sold more CALLs on his BellSouth but transferred other stocks so we could do the same with some of his other stocks. Wally once asked me, "How much money to you think I lost because I didn't sell covered calls before now?"

And this is why I included this story here. There are a lot of people who own stocks that have no idea what a covered call is, or how it works. It is not unusual to be able to make from 3% to %12 or even more on a stock just by adding covered calls to a portfolio's strategies. Of course, not all stocks are good candidates for covered call writing, but many are.

Don't Leave Money on the Table

Fast forward to year 2017. Just before the first edition of this book, I went to my local pub to have an afternoon refreshment. As often happens, I struck up a conversation with a fellow sitting next to me. His name is Carl. Carl was retirement age, so I asked him what line of work did he do most of his life. He told me he retired six years ago from Georgia Power Company, after working for them 41 years. I have owned some Southern Company stock, so knew it that Georgia Power was a part of the parent company (and others, see below.)

Southern Company is one of the largest energy providers in the United States and 162nd on the Fortune 500 listing of the largest U. S. corporations. It has more than 500,000 shareholders (NYSE: SO) and has been traded since September 30, 1949.

Southern Company subsidiaries are building the first new nuclear units in the U.S. in 30 years at Plant Vogtle near Augusta, Georgia; building a 21st-century coal facility in Kemper County, Mississippi; are operating or developing renewable solar, wind and biomass facilities across the U.S.

Four retail electric companies: Alabama Power, Georgia Power, Gulf Power, Mississippi Power, serve 120,000 square miles (310,000 km^2) in four states. Southern Power serves wholesale electricity customers across the U.S. Southern Company Gas serves utility customers in seven states.

I asked Carl if he accumulated any of the Southern Company stock during his tenure with them, and his voice showed excitement when he answered with a big smile, "Oh yeah, I bought every share I could the whole time and they did a matching plan for employees that let me get many extra shares. I own about 43,500 shares of Southern Company."

"I'll bet all those good dividends they pay make your retirement a lot of fun, huh?" I asked. Carl gets thousands of dollars in dividends each quarter from his shares, and he couldn't be happier. I asked him if he ever sold any covered calls to add to his money from his stock holdings.

"Well, I don't know anything about that," he said. From his tone and lack of interest, I could tell he had no idea what a covered call was. I told him I wrote books about stocks and options investments and that he might want to talk to someone about making money selling call options on his stock. Carl politely changed the subject, and I knew he knew nothing about covered calls, and did not want to learn, so I dropped it. After all, I was a stranger to him and he didn't know me. I live near Atlanta, GA and it is the custom here, and just about everywhere else, for strangers not to be too imposing on subjects as personal as another's financial situation.

I had not traded or looked up Southern Company in several years. When I got home, I looked up Southern Company to see how much dividend they pay. Here's a recent page from finance.yahoo.com on symbol SO (Southern Company): (Note: *Dividend & Yield*: $2.24 (4.51%))

The Southern Company (SO)

source: finance.yahoo.com

NYSE - Nasdaq Real Time Price. Currency in USD

49.60 -0.06 (-0.12%)

As of 2:19PM. Market open

date: April 13, 2017

Summary	Conversations	Statistics	Profile	Financials	Options	Holders	Historical Data	Analysts

Previous Close	49.66	Market Cap	49.37B
Open	49.68	Beta	0.04
Bid	0.00 x	PE Ratio (TTM)	19.45
Ask	0.00 x	EPS (TTM)	2.55
Day's Range	49.31 - 49.68	Earnings Date	Feb 1, 2017 - Feb 6, 2017
52 Week Range	46.20 - 54.64	Dividend & Yield	2.24 (4.51%)
Volume	3,458,216	Ex-Dividend Date	N/A
Avg. Volume	5,318,829	1y Target Est	50.71

Trade prices are not sourced from all markets

Southern Company is a Fortune 500 company. It trades in high volume, an average of 5.318 million shares per day. Over the last year, the range of the stock price has been from $46.20 to $54.64 per share. Although, used here for illustration only, you can see clearly it is the sort of stock that is fairly low risk, and a good candidate to write calls on.

Carl has 43,500 shares, so at $49.60 a share, that's = $2,157,600. Carl had told me he never took a dime out of his retirement plan, and the stock had split twice, giving him more shares, and that he had all the dividends reinvested automatically to buy more shares. If you look on the previous page the annual yield of the dividends is 4.51%. This means that Carl gets (.0451 x 2,157,600) = $93,307.76 a year in cash stock dividends now! Not shabby!

Carl (and that isn't his real name of course) will probably never learn how much more he could be making from his stock, if he only knew and used the covered call strategy. Below, I will put the matrix for SO covered calls, so we can see some of the possibilities – while we practice your new found knowledge of how to use covered calls to increase your income:

	Last X	Net Chng	Bid X	Ask X		
❯	49.46 N	-.20	49.46 N	49.47 N		

❯ Trade Grid **SOUTHERN COMPANY**

⌄ Option Chain   Filter: **Off** ⌐   Spread: **Single** ⌐   Layout: **Net Change, Probability OTM, Last X** ⌐

		CALLS			Strikes: 8 ⏷	
Net Chng ⌐	Prob.OTM ⌐	Last X ⌐	Bid X	Ask X	Exp	Strike
❯ 21 APR 17 (8) 100						
⌄ 19 MAY 17 (36) 100						
0	17.00%	4.50 W	3.40 X	3.80 X	19 MAY 17	46
-.12	19.93%	2.73 Z	2.55 C	2.63 X	19 MAY 17	47
+.19	31.46%	1.84 C	1.74 C	1.82 X	19 MAY 17	48
0	46.12%	1.12 Z	1.01 C	1.09 B	19 MAY 17	49
-.04	64.23%	.58 A	.49 X	.58 C	19 MAY 17	50
-.02	93.80% ➡ .06 C		.04 Q	.08 M	19 MAY 17	52.5
0	97.80%	.02 Q	0 P	.05 C	19 MAY 17	55
0	98.90%	.56 B	0 P	.03 M	19 MAY 17	57.5

As you can see from this SO CALL Options matrix, the 52.50- strike CALL that expires in (36) days, last sold for 0.06, which is .06 x 100 = $6. Selling 435 (43,500/100) of them would yield ($6 x 435) = $2610. Note: SO is currently trading at $49.46 per share. So, Carl, would have made $72.50 a day average for the next 36 days.

Now see if you can compute the answer to this question: If Carl had selected to sell the 50-strike CALL option, how much premium would he collect?

Answer: The "last trade" for the 50-strike CALL is .58 or $58 premium per option. If he sold the maximum amount of covered calls, that's 435 of them @ $58 each, so the total credited to his account would have been: $58 times 435 = $25,230. That isn't bad for a time period of only 36 days!

Here's another practice question for you. Had Carl sold those 50-strike CALLs and they been exercised, his stocks would have been sold at the strike price of $50 per share, plus he would get the option premium of $25,230. What would have been his total net gain?

Answer: note: Since the CALLs were exercised, this means on the expiration date (in 36 days on the 19th of May 2017), the stock price would have been somewhere at $50 or more. Since the stock is currently trading at $49.46, he would profit .54 per share = (43500 x $.54) = $23,490. Adding that to his collected option premium of $25,230, would be a total of $48,720.

 I would have advised Carl to just sell the 52.50 CALLs, since he does not want to sell his stock. Look at the option matrix again in the column labeled "Prob OTM", which means "Probability the option will expire out-of-the-money" meaning the chances he would NOT be called away (his stock sold). The Prob OTM is 93.80%, a relatively safe number. (In case you are a 'math head' kind of person, that Prob OTM is computed (all done for you, transparently) using the volatility of the stock, it's current price, and with the Black-Scholes formula using the stock price distance from the strike price of the option sold, and the number of days until expiration of the option.) It is good to preview the "Prob OTM", so you can have at least some idea of the chances of the option being exercised. Other factors, *not* in Prob OTM factor, are the market in general (bull/bear/neutral), and any dividend dates, and fundamental information relating to your stock.

Chapter 3: Using Covered Calls to Reduce the Purchase Price of a Stock

When an investor buys a stock and immediately sells a CALL, this is called a BUY-WRITE. To illustrate how this works, I'll use a real stock with real values. Apple shares are the most widely held stock in the USA among investors ages 35 to 64 years old. Of course these numbers will change everyday, so by the time you read this, they will all change but the strategy and purpose of the BUY-WRITE will remain as it is now. An investor wants to own a stock and, if possible, find an edge to own it just a little cheaper than the market.

Here's the example: On April 13, 2017 AAPL stock is trading at $141.05.

Apple Inc. (AAPL)
NasdaqGS - NasdaqGS Delayed Price. Currency in USD

source: financial.yahoo.com

141.05 -0.75 (-0.53%)
As of April 13 4:00PM EDT. 2017

Summary

Previous Close	141.80	Market Cap	740.02B	
Open	141.91	Beta	1.44	
Bid	141.02 x 400	PE Ratio (TTM)	16.93	
Ask	141.10 x 1000	EPS (TTM)	8.33	
Day's Range	141.05 - 142.38	Earnings Date	Apr 24, 2017 - Apr 28, 2017	
52 Week Range	89.47 - 145.46	Dividend & Yield	2.28 (1.59%)	
Volume	17,822,880	Ex-Dividend Date	N/A	
Avg. Volume	26,609,591	1y Target Est	147.61	

1D 5D 1M 6M YTD 1Y 2Y 5Y **10Y** MAX   Interactive chart

APPLE TEN-YEAR PRICE CHART

141.05

$18.82

As you can see on the AAPL price chart, the stock was $18.82 in July of 2007 and is now at $141.05. You may also notice that the price at times has been very volatile. Another remarkable thing about AAPL is that it has huge cash reserves of just over (as of January 2017) $246 Billion!

Now let's study this example of how an investor can use a BUY-WRITE to own AAPL. Let's suppose she buys 100 shares @ $141.05, and then sells a CALL option. Here's the matrix with the AAPL CALL options:

	Last X	Net Chng	Bid X	Ask X
❯	141.05 Q	-.75	141.02 P	141.10 P

❯ Trade Grid   **Apple Option Matrix: CALLS on 13 April 2017**

⌄ Option Chain   Filter: **Off** ⌐   Spread: **Single** ⌐   Layout: **Net Change, Probability OTM, Last X** ⌐

		CALLS				Strikes: 8 ▼	
	Net Chng ⌐	Prob.OT... ⌐	Last X ⌐	Bid X	Ask X	Exp	Strike
⌄ 16 JUN 17	(63) 100						
	-.44	12.79%	16.66 C	16.50 X	16.75 T	16 JUN 17	125
	-.50	20.52%	12.25 Q	12.05 M	12.30 X	16 JUN 17	130
	-.17	32.36%	8.38 C	8.05 H	8.25 H	16 JUN 17	135
	-.35	48.64%	5.05 Q	4.85 M	5.00 X	16 JUN 17	140
➡	-.34	66.06%	2.66 X	2.62 Q	2.68 W	16 JUN 17	145
	-.20	80.57%	1.30 C	1.26 Q	1.30 H	16 JUN 17	150
	-.11	89.99%	.60 Q	.57 H	.60 H	16 JUN 17	155
	-.04	94.92%	.29 Z	.27 Q	.29 M	16 JUN 17	160

Look on the line with the black horizontal arrow on the left side: This tells us the bid/ask on the 145-strike CALL is 2.62/2.68 last traded at 2.66. Selling this CALL means your account is credited $2.62 for each of 100 AAPL shares, a total of $266.00. Since you just bought a hundred shares at $141.05, and you got a credit of $266 for selling (writing) the option, your new net price per share is ($141.05 minus 2.66) = $138.39. It is 63 days until this 145-strike option expires. If it gets exercised, your stock is sold at $145/share and your profit is:

$145 minus your net purchase price of $138.39 = $6.61 per share or $661. If the option isn't exercised (meaning on expiration in 63 days AAPL price is below the strike of 145), you are long the 100 shares at a net of $138.39. After the option expires, you can write another CALL and reduce your cost basis even more. If you keep doing this again and again, you will continue to reduce your cost basis for the stock. This means even if the AAPL stock doesn't go up, you will continue to make money by writing (selling) the CALLs over time. So you see, by using the covered call strategy, the market doesn't have to go UP for you to make money.

Of course you are at risk of the price of AAPL stock going down, and if the AAPL ever goes OVER the strike price of the option(s) you sell, you will be called away and NOT make any rise *over* the strike-price of the CALL. There's the old adage: Everything nice has its price, and the "price you pay" for selling the CALL is you give up any rise in price over the strike-price of the CALL. If you are expecting some news that could be very bullish for your stock, you might want to NOT sell any CALLs until your view changes. Also, note that AAPL stock currently (at time of trade example) pays a 1.59% annual yield dividend.

So you get the dividend, hopefully some rise in the stock price, and the premiums you collect from selling the covered CALL options, a "triple-whammy" of income. If, on a transaction such as this BUY-WRITE, the investor was buying AAPL for the long term, he or she might continue selling CALLs some or all of the time. If, on the other hand an investor thought the stock might rise above the strike of 145, collecting the $2.66 premium on selling the CALL could be considered as "insurance" in case the stock did not go up.

Another variation you can use is to SELL A HIGHER STRIKE PRICE option. Go back and look at the AAPL CALL option matrix again: You see the 150-strike is priced at 1.30, which means the "called away" net would be 150 + 1.30 = 151.30, profiting about $10.25 per share or at total of $1025 . Your net cost per share would be $141.05 minus 1.30 = $139.75.

Now, just for practice, use the 155-strike: It can be sold for about .60, so the net cost of stock would be $141.05 minus .60 = $140.45. If you were "called away" (the price of AAPL was 155 or higher, you would profit: 155 – 140.45 = $14.55 per share (total: $1455).

I used these illustrations, so you can see how stock traders, as compared to long-term buy and hold investors, might consider the use of a covered-call strategy. Remember to use your broker's paper-trading free account to practice some of these strategies. You need confidence in both your ability to plan and use the strategy AND you need practice using the trading software. Think of your paper-trading account, as your "flight simulator" for learning to trade. You'll be astounded how fast you can "learn by doing" if you take advantage of this paper-trading account and use it to practice.

More Questions & Answers

Question: How do I select the STRIKE PRICE for covered-call selling (writing)?

Answer: Assuming you want to pick a STRIKE that probably won't have you sell your stock, you try to select the highest STRIKE-PRICE that still has enough premium (payoff) to make it worth your efforts. Sometimes, during times of low volatility, the option CALL premiums may not be high enough. Whether or not you are trading in a tax-deferred account is also a consideration. If you are NOT in a tax-deferred account, you may be subject to capital gains tax – consult tax advice for more information. In your trading software, as you look up option prices and strikes in the option matrix, you can set up a box that shows "Prob OTM" (Probability this option will expire Out-Of-The-Money.) If you don't know how, get help from your broker; this is easy to do. If the "Prob OTM" says 85%, that means the mathematical odds are, 85% your option might not be exercised. There is no guarantee of this happening, but the trading program uses the volatility of your stock, the amount it is OTM, and the time until the option expires to compute this indicator. You should keep in mind, this number does not consider all the factors that influence the price of your stock. Some traders, who may not care if they must sell the stock, will sell CALL STRIKES closer to the trading price in order to collect more premium. Other more conservative traders, might not be willing to sell a CALL unless the Prob OTM is a set percentage; for example 80% or 90%. This may sound complicated in the beginning, but using the "Prob. OTM" parameter is easy and it will become second-nature to you quickly. Keep in mind that many stocks are much more volatile in price than others; the premiums on stock prices that move quicker and more often, will be higher than lower volatility stock prices. Having a CALL you have sold (written) being exercised is neither a "good" or "bad" thing; it all depends on how much premium you try to get and how willing (or not) you are to sell the stock. There are situations when you may *want* to sell your stock – or you don't care one way or the other. If you are trading in a tax-deferred account, there are no tax consequences, so the decision could be much easier, as you can buy the stock back immediately or perhaps later at perhaps a lower price. If you are trading with stock you inherited consult a tax professional or other reliable source to determine your *cost basis* for your stock.

Question: What is the minimum amount I should sell (write) a CALL option for?

Answer: You have already learned that each option represents 100 shares of a stock. You cannot write a covered CALL unless you own (or are buying) a hundred shares. There is no "set answer" to this question, it all depends on how much you stand to gain from selling the CALL option. If you only own 100 shares and you sell a CALL for a small amount, for example .10 ($10) or less, you might think this isn't worth the effort, after paying a $2 commission to net $8.00. On the other hand, if you own 20,000 shares and sell 200 calls, you would collect 200 times $8 = $1600. While the rate of return would be the same for $8 as it is $1600, the motivation to do it might not be the same. Again, there is no set "right" or "wrong."

If you are new to all of this., you will notice that over time that you "get to know" the price behavior of individual stocks. For example your shares of Apple (AAPL) are much more volatile than your shares of Southern Company (SO). Shares of AAPL can vary quite a bit on things like earnings reports or new product announcements, while shares of a widely traded, stable utility stock (like SO) do not normally have as much price volatility. This is why you should have a list of stocks in your "watch list" in your account to monitor. If you are a beginner, it is probably best you stick with large cap stocks that are widely traded and household names. "Hot story" stocks, and new stocks called "IPO's" (Initial Public Offerings) can be more risky. Remember, when something sounds "too good to be true," it probably is.

Question: What happens if I own a stock, have written covered-calls on it, and the market crashes?

Answer: The bad news is the price of your stock is going down. The good news is that your covered call is now cheap and will probably expire worthless. If you decide to sell your underlying stock, you should buy the covered call back and close the position. If you do not close your position (and you have a choice), you will risk a price reversal and encounter risks by holding this "naked call." Unless your very long-term outlook on your stock has changed for a good reason, just wait for things to settle down, and continue the same strategies you've been using all along. One of the master investors of all time, Warren Buffett, has said, "The stock market is a way of transferring money from the impatient to the patient investor." Often, for the long-term investor using these market sell-offs is an opportunity to buy more of a good stock at a lower price (better value investing).

One thing that often alarms new investors (and many of the old ones) is to be watching some news story and/or stock news channel and hear some talking-head anchor say something like, "The DOW is unexpectedly falling with double-digit losses!" When the stock market DOW average is near 20,000, a "double digit loss" of the DOW average could be -30 points. Let's put that into perspective: 30 points of loss of 20,000 is only .15%, hardly a move at all. But that announcer or writer, who often has little or no experience in stocks, has to "report a headline." Keep your perspective when all about you are losing theirs, and you may find opportunity instead of turmoil.

> *"Over the long-term, the stock market news will be good. In the 20th century the United States endured two world wars and other traumatic and expensive military conflicts; the Depression; a dozen or so recessions and financial panics; oil shocks; a flu epidemic; and the resignation of a disgraced president. Yet the Dow rose from 66 to 11,491." –* *Warren Buffett*

Remember to get your FREE BONUS CHAPTER:

To get the free BONUS chapter, just send me an email at Don@WriteThisDown.com and put COVERED CALL in the subject line. This free information contains tips for dividend stock selection, selecting good candidates for covered-call selling, and stocks with DRIPs. If you have a question or comment, just drop me an email; I'd be glad to hear from you.

Chapter 4: Get Paid to Buy Stocks
The Cash-Secured PUT

What if you were in the city waiting on a traffic light to change so you could cross the road, and someone came up to you and said, "I'll pay you $20 to cross the road when the light changes." This would be an offer for you to get paid to do what you already were going to do anyway. This is what happens when you sell a CASH-SECURED PUT option.

This time, I'll use a fictional stock to illustrate: Let's suppose you have been wanting to buy shares in the XYZ company, and the shares are above what you are willing to pay. In this hypothetical, suppose XYZ was trading for $50 per share but you have decided you would be certainly willing to buy it at $45 per share. On the option matrix you find if you sell a 45-strike PUT option on XYZ, you can collect a premium of 1.50. As the SELLER of this PUT option, you will be OBLIGATED to buy 100 shares IF - at or before expiration - your sold option is exercised. If the stock is trading at or below the strike price at expiration, you are *obligated* to buy at the price you wanted of $45 a share. You have been credited in your account $150 ($1.50 per share) when you sold the 45-strike PUT option. Your net price for the stock would be the strike price of 45 less the credit of 1.50 = a net cost of 43.50 for the 100 shares you are assigned. If prices do not go down to or below the strike, you will not be assigned and you just keep the $150 credit. Once the option expires, you can SELL another PUT or not, as you please. You must have the money in your account to BUY the shares at the strike before you use this strategy. This cash in your account is the *security* for the possible trade when you SELL the PUT option, thus the name: CASH-SECURED PUT strategy.

Let's review:
When you own stock and write (sell) a CALL, this is a COVERED CALL.
When you sell a PUT on a stock you do NOT own, you must have cash in your account to buy the stock IF the option is exercised (CASH-SECURED PUT).

The seller of the COVERED CALL is OBLIGATED to SELL the stock if the stock price is <u>OVER</u> the strike at expiration (and possibly before expiration).

The seller of the CASH-SECURED PUT is OBLIGATED to BUY the stock if the price is <u>BELOW</u> the strike at expiration (and possibly before expiration).

Now, for practice let's use the AAPL stock example and perform a CASH SECURED PUT strategy, so you can see how it works:

You recall AAPL is trading at $141.05 per share. Before, we studied the CALLS; this time we will look at the AAPL option matrix for PUTS, and examine possibilities using the CASH-SECURED PUT strategy:

AAPL CURRENT PRICE: 141.05

Apple 16JUN17 MATRIX PUTS   PUTS Expiration (63) days

Strike	Bid X	Ask X	Net Chng	Prob.OT...	Last X
125	.64 Q	.65 Q	-.08	88.47%	.58
130	1.19 W	1.23 M	-.02	80.36%	1.17
135	2.27 H	2.31 P	+.05	67.71%	2.25
140	4.10 C	4.20 C	+.05	51.29%	4.00
145	6.80 M	6.95 T	+.05	34.14%	6.65

Let's suppose you want to buy AAPL stock but think the price is too high. With the stock currently at 141.05, you reason that you would buy the stock at 130 and be glad to do so. You have funds in your account to buy it. If you are sure you would buy at 130, you could SELL a 130-strike PUT option for 1.17. Since each option represents 100 shares the premium (price) of the option is $117.00. You sell the PUT option and the premium is immediately credited to your account. The date of this option is 16 JUN 17, which means June 16, 2017 is the date the option expires, 63 days away.

If the option PUTS the stock to you, at expiration the stock is at or below the 130-strike, you will own 100 shares at a net price of 130 minus the 1.17 = $128.83.

If at expiration the price is at or above 130, the option expires worthless; this means you keep the $117 credit. And now, you are free to sell another CASH-SECURED PUT if you choose. This is a great way to "get paid for what you would do anyway."

More Getting Paid for What You Would Do Anyway

If you have a stock in your portfolio that you want to sell but you are not in a hurry to do so – you probably have a target price in mind just above where it's trading now. It is just human nature to want that 'little bit more'. Well there is a way to sort of 'have your cake and eat it too.' Write covered calls on the stock and use a strike-price at which you would be glad to sell the stock. The result will be one of two outcomes, and you win in either case. The stock is called away at the strike as the price rises to or above the strike price, OR you keep the premium from selling the OTM call and the net result is that decreases your cost basis for the stock. The only thing you 'give up' is any gain the stock might have made above the price where you would have sold it anyway! If any these possibilities are not acceptable to you, don't do the trade. There are two other sage sayings: "There's is always 20-20 genius in hindsight." and "There are bulls, bears, and pigs!" *You must fully understand the best case, worst case, and probable outcome of each trade before you commit.* You will never be able to predict the future with certainty but you can understand and accept the consequences of each trade you choose to execute.

Of course, if you fear a stock price is vulnerable and you've decided to sell, you will usually do it at the first opportunity. But there are times, when you might need to sell a stock and you are in no hurry. For example, you may have 300 shares of SO, Southern Company, that you wish to liquidate and use the money to purchase another stock, or perhaps you have other reasons like a cash withdrawal from your account. If you are not in a hurry and your opinion is that the stock price is unlikely to drop over the next few weeks, you can sell an ITM (In-The-Money) or ATM (At-The-Money) CALL option to try and make a few more dollars.

This is the SO option matrix for the 19 MAY 17 CALLs. I prefer to use real stocks and real quotes in examples when possible, but this means you must remember 'where in time' these examples are working. This SO example (as noted in the graphic) is the 19 MAY 17 (The options expire in (34) days on May 19, 2017, and the date of the quotes is April 14, 2017, 34 days before these CALLs expire.

>	Last X	Net Chng	Bid X	Ask X	Size
	49.42 N	-.24	49.02 P	49.58 P	1 x 1

> Trade Grid **SOUTHERN COMPANY TRADING @ 49.42 DATE: April 14, 2017**

˅ Option Chain   Filter: **Off** ˏ Spread: **Single** ˏ Layout: **Net Change, Probability OTM, Last X** ˏ

CALLS   Strikes: 8 ▼

Net Chng ˏ	Prob.OTM ˏ	Last X ˏ	Bid X	Ask X	Exp	Strike
> 21 APR 17	(6)	100				
˅ 19 MAY 17	(34)	100	**CALL OPTIONS: EXPIRE IN (34) DAYS on May 19, 2017**			
0	16.20%	4.50 W	3.30 X	3.80 X	19 MAY 17	46
-.12	21.74%	2.73 Z	2.54 X	2.68 M	19 MAY 17	47
+.08	31.64%	1.73 I	1.71 B	1.80 B	19 MAY 17	48
0	46.54%	1.12 Z	.98 B	1.07 B	19 MAY 17	49
-.11	64.88%	.51 N	.48 X	.57 B	19 MAY 17	50
-.04	94.75%	.04 Q	.01 X	.09 M	19 MAY 17	52.5
0	98.26%	.02 Q	0 P	.04 M	19 MAY 17	55
0	99.26%	.56 B	0 P	.02 M	19 MAY 17	57.5

Sell the 50 strike for $51 (.51) and, if the stock is called away, make a gain of (.58) $58 for a total of $109. If the stock at expiration is not $50 or greater, you just keep the $51 you made selling the CALL.   The 50-strike CALL, which is .58 above the present trading price, is bid/ask at .48/.57 and last traded for .51 ($51.) The higher strikes in the matrix of 52.5, 55, and 57.5 have premiums so small that there isn't enough money there worth trading it. This is a good time to show you an 'abnormality' on this matrix: Look at the 57.5 strike: the bid/ask is 0/.02, but the "Last X" (meaning: last traded) is at .56. It has been a while since that option was traded, so the "Last X" is not between the bid/ask, but still it was "the last price at which it traded. The lesson to be learned here is that sometimes the numbers in a matrix won't appear to make sense. So when you see anomalies, there is usually a reason for them. All the options in the 19 MAY 17 are relatively cheap because they expire so soon. They have very little "time value." Options with those same strikes, that are in the more distant future ("farther out") will have higher prices (more time-value.)

The Collar Strategy

The COLLAR is a very specific strategy that can be very useful. Let's say you own 100 shares of AAPL stock at $141.05. Our market view on the price of AAPL is that the stock could sell off and cause you losses over the next two months. You feel this is a strong possibility, but do not want to liquidate (sell) the stock. Use a COLLAR for protection. We'll use the same options matrix of the last AAPL examples: The 16JUN17 CALLS and PUTS.

Sell the 150-stike CALL for 1.30 AND
Buy the 130-strike PUT for 1.17

The credit for the call is $130 and the cost (debit) for the PUT $117, so you get a small net credit of (130-117) = $13 to your account.

You are SELLING A CALL and using that money to BUY A PUT in order to protect the downside on the stock you own. This is a COLLAR. Practice this strategy by trying out different CALL and PUT strikes. Usually, this is a low cost way of protecting the downside.

APPLE CALLS   Strikes: 8 ▼

Net Chng	Prob.OT...	Last X	Bid X	Ask X	Exp	Strike
∨ 16 JUN 17	(63) 100					
-.44	12.79%	16.66 C	16.50 X	16.75 T	16 JUN 17	125
-.50	20.52%	12.25 Q	12.05 M	12.30 X	16 JUN 17	130
-.17	32.36%	8.38 C	8.05 H	8.25 H	16 JUN 17	135
-.35	48.64%	5.05 Q	4.85 M	5.00 X	16 JUN 17	140
-.34	66.06%	2.66 X	2.62 Q	2.68 W	16 JUN 17	145
-.20	80.57% ➡	1.30 C	1.26 Q	1.30 H	16 JUN 17	150
-.11	89.99%	.60 Q	.57 H	.60 H	16 JUN 17	155
-.04	94.92%	.29 Z	.27 Q	.29 M	16 JUN 17	160

Apple 16JUN17 MATRIX PUTS   PUTS   Expiration (63) days

Strike	Bid X	Ask X	Net Chng	Prob.OT...	Last X
125	.64 Q	.65 Q	-.08	88.47%	.58
130	1.19 W	1.23 M	-.02	80.36%	1.17
135	2.27 H	2.31 P	+.05	67.71%	2.25
140	4.10 C	4.20 C	+.05	51.29%	4.00
145	6.80 M	6.95 T	+.05	34.14%	6.65

COLLAR

You Own the AAPL Stock at 141.05
Write (SELL) a covered 150-STRIKE CALL for 1.30
and BUY a 130-STRIKE PUT for 1.17. You get a net credit of $13.

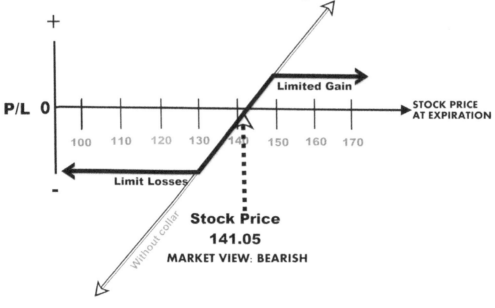

Chapter 5: Selecting Stocks to use With Covered Calls

This first list of stocks you might consider to use with the covered-calls strategy is a list of well-known stocks, all large caps (big companies), and they all pay decent dividends. Options and shares are traded in great volume on NYSE or NASDAQ. Some of them have the shorter-term weekly options available.

Symbol	Company	Dividend %	Trading Price per Share
WMT	Wal-Mart Stores	2.70%	74.94
K	Kellogg Co.	2.90%	72.42
JNJ	Johnson & Johnson	2.60%	121.76
MMM	3M	2.50%	191.5
PEP	PepsiCo	2.70%	113.43
GWW	W.W.Grainger	2.50%	195.15
APD	Air Products & Chemicals	2.80%	137.3
EIX	Edison International	2.70%	80.6
RTN	Raytheon Co.	2.10%	154.04
TXN	Texas Instruments	2.50%	79.81
MDT	Medtronic, Inc.	2.10%	80.48
DLR	Digital Realty Trust	3.30%	112.88
WM	Waste Management	2.30%	73.38
PG	Procter & Gamble	3.10%	88.62
T	AT&T	4.90%	39.93
VZ	Verizon	4.90%	47.25
TGT	Target	4.40%	54.78
ABBV	AbbVie Inc.	4.00%	63.82
MSFT	Microsoft	2.30%	66.42
SO	Southern Company	4.60%	49.98

This list was partially compiled using a stock-screener at dividend.com, a web site that has information on dividend stocks. Not only do these stocks pay fair dividends, but they all have a ten-year history of increasing dividend payments. There are many places to find reliable lists like this one. Remember to send for your bonus chapter by sending me an email to Don@WriteThisDown.com with COVERED CALLS in the subject line, and I'll send you an updated list of where you can find this information and more.

Symbol	Company	Dividend %	Trading Price per Share
TROW	T. Rowe Price	3.20%	71.79
VFC	V.F. Corporation	3.00%	55.85
CLX	Clorox Co.	2.40%	134.29
KO	Coca-Cola Co.	3.40%	43.07
SYY	Sysco Corp	2.50%	52.2
DUK	Duke Energy	4.20%	82.21
KMB	Kimberly-Clark	3.00%	129.96
AFL	Aflac	2.30%	73.99
ED	Consolidated Edison	3.50%	79.09
EMR	Emerson Electric	3.30%	59
CB	Chubb Corp	2.00%	135.48
ABT	Abbott Labs	2.40%	43.53
CL	Colgate-Palmolive	2.20%	73.02
LNT	Alliant Energy	3.20%	39.96
ADM	Archer Daniels Midland Co.	2.90%	44.81
CINF	Cincinnati Financial	2.80%	70.18
ESS	Essex Property Trust	3.00%	235.49
GPC	Genuine Parts	2.90%	93.11
GIS	General Mills	3.30%	57.73
XY	Occidental Petroleum	4.90%	61.86
OKE	ONEOK Inc.	4.60%	53.53
PNR	Pentair Inc.	2.20%	62.57
QCOM	Qualcomm, Inc.	4.30%	52.5
XEL	Xcel Energy	3.20%	44.83
CAH	Cardinal Health	2.50%	72.5
IBM	IBM Corp	3.50%	160.38
SJM	The J.M. Smucker Company	2.40%	126.58
CNP	CenterPoint Energy	3.80%	28.12

Dividend Trade-Offs

While all stocks have risks and are subject to market cycles, stocks like those on this list are generally speaking, conservative plays. Please note that FDIC insured CD rates are near 2.5 to 3%, while a great many stocks on this list pay a little more. This is not a coincidence. Stocks (like those on the list) are a little more risky than bank CD's, so they pay a little more return. There are stocks that are paying 10% or more dividends but they are not on this list because they are much more risky. My advice it to stay away from those high-yield dividends and the associated risk of those stocks; consider it a red flag.

There are growth stocks like Apple that pay lower dividends while also holding the possibility of good rise in stock price. While a utility company like Southern Company may not have tremendous capital gains (increases in its stock price), it does offer stability and a higher yield dividend, plus it has stock-options available.

If you only have funds for a few stocks, you may prefer less risk and go with good-name reliable dividend paying companies. If you have enough funds, you will probably consider adding some growth stocks and writing calls on those (like Apple, Facebook, Google, Intel, or other such stocks.) Risk is always commensurate with gain; there is no "free lunch."

If you already own stocks of various risk levels and dividend payments, of course you can write CALL options on them. If you are just starting out, you might be better off to stay with a good steady dividend stock and use the covered-call strategy with it.

While not at the time this book is published, CD rates could reach 9 or 10% or higher; under that scenario good dividend stocks should have a yield slightly higher than the CD's that are federally insured (FDIC.) In the late 1970's bank CD's yielded as high as 16 to 18%. Mortgage rates for houses, at that time were 12 to 14% and higher. During those times, many people switched out of stocks and put their money into these historically high-yield FDIC insured certificates of deposit. It could be years before we see rates that high again, if ever.

Stock Price Volatility and the Price of Options

Of course the prices of CALL options you write on your stocks will vary. On steady-priced, fair dividend stocks, CALL options, relatively speaking, are not priced as high as on growth stocks like Apple, Facebook, or Netflix. Why do options sell for a higher price on growth-type stocks? It is because their price varies more in both amplitude and frequency than good steady dividend stocks. Investors imply that these growth stocks will have bigger price moves than other stocks. This implied fact adds what is termed *implied volatility* to the options price. *Implied Volatility* is normally written as Implied vol, or simply IV%. This implied volatility (IV%) value can go up, if a stock is rising fast, or dropping fast. The more a stock's price is varying (up or down, and how much), the higher will be the IV% of its options.

It is for this reason, that growth stocks have options that sell at a higher premium, than less volatile stocks. Of course, the more volatile a stock's price is, the more probability that it could move through your covered-call's strike price. The trade-off is, that you get to sell it for a higher premium. Again, risk is commensurate with gain (still no free lunch.)

The other large component of the option's premium is *time value*. The longer until an options expiration date, the more time premium the option has. Now, here's another trade-off: The longer an option has until it expires, the more money you can sell it for, but also this longer time until expiration means a greater chance (probability) that your option could be exercised. This may seem a bit complicated if you are new to options, but as you gain experience with specific stocks, you will come to know a "fair price" for a stock's options and how it relates with the price of the stock.

When you are trading a stock with a more steady reliable price (low volatility or low-beta), you might be more comfortable selling a more distant (longer time until option expiration) option and collecting a higher premium.

Please see Chapter 7 for more information about stock's dividend reinvestment plans (DRIP's.) If you want more information on selecting growth stocks, there are many examples in my book for stock market beginners: *Stock Market for Beginners Paycheck Freedom*

Chapter 6
Opening Your Online Trading Account

I've included a small chapter here in case you are new to trading and need to open an account. If you are already up and trading, you might wish to skip this section.

The application process is very simple. The brokerage company will have you fill out a few forms to open the account, execute a (separate) margin agreement, and you will add an options agreement to your account. These applications will gather information on you to make sure you are credit worthy and that you have the experience and understanding to trade your account at the various levels they may approve.

When a person opens an account, they are assigned one of several option approval levels supposedly based on the option trader's knowledge and needs.

In many instances, option traders opening an account are either not aware of these levels, or they will not be sure which levels they may apply to trade. After reading and studying this book, you won't have any problem going to intermediate levels. Experienced investors often qualify for all levels when they open the account, whether they intend to trade them initially or not; this keeps you from having to do more paperwork later, when you do wish to trade them. Anyone who is uncertain of their option approval level should read more about it (at OIC), or

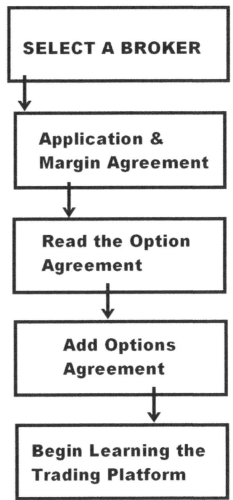

SELECT A BROKER

Application & Margin Agreement

Read the Option Agreement

Add Options Agreement

Begin Learning the Trading Platform

contact his or her broker to find out which level of option approval their account has.

Normally, there are four option approval levels. There is no official standard of what strategies could be traded at which level. The categories described below are typical levels used by most trading companies. A level 4 can trade all four categories, a level 3 can also trade 1 and 2 but not 4, and so on.

Option Approval Levels	Strategies Approved
Level 1	Covered Call, Long Protective Puts
Level 2	Long call/put
Level 3	Spreads
Level 4	Uncovered or Naked

If you only want to buy CALLS and PUTS, and sell covered CALLS, a margin agreement is not required. If you want to place debit and credit spreads, you'll need to have the margin account. To trade more advanced strategies, the brokerage company needs to know you have the experience and financial resources to trade these higher levels.

You should read the technical brochure carefully – *Characteristics and Risks of Standardized Options* and make sure you understand the risky aspects of this type trading. You shouldn't have any problem understanding this brochure and the options agreement once you have read this book.

It is, by law, the brokers responsibility to gather this information on your financial resources and trading experience; most use a group of standardized questions on the applications.

You can read more about the LEVELS at the OIC.com website if you wish. Understand which of these levels are suitable for you before you apply for the account so you can communicate clearly with your trading company.

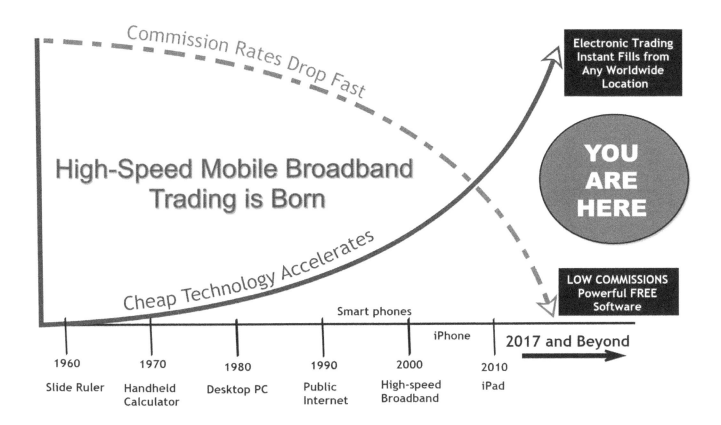

Trading from mobile devices with free vendor software and the lowest commissions in history is fast becoming the norm for individual investors.

The Functions of Your Online Broker

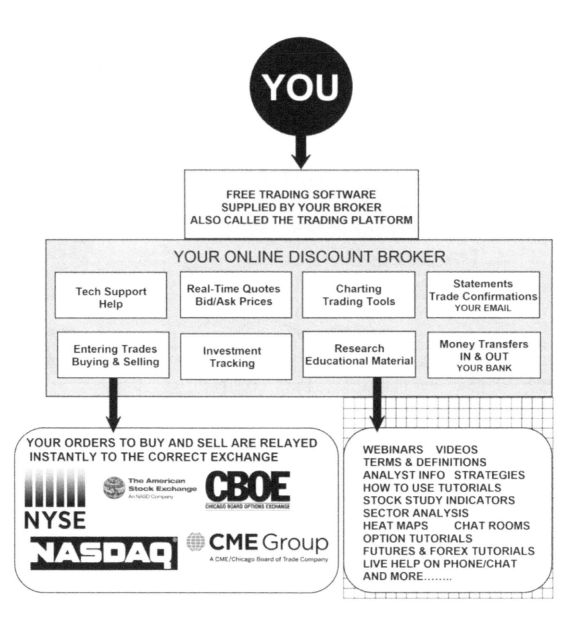

Tech support: It is quite normal if you are new to your broker - that you will have some questions on how to install and operate the software, a.k.a. "The trading platform." There are scores of training videos, articles, webinars, and written instructions either on line / in a manual to help you learn to operate the software. It is imperative that you open a practice session (paper trading account) so you can familiarize yourself with all operating aspects of the software and to learn about the services your broker offers. Some of the brokers have 'for fee' services; my advice it that until you gain a lot of experience, you do not sign up for any of those. You will find more than enough to explore and learn without buying additional services. You should try and find answers to your questions by viewing videos and reading instructions as much as you can. When you get stuck, phone your broker and they will get you going again. As a courtesy, it is the custom that you should be as quick and specific as you can when you phone them for help. Brokers usually have a text chat help service also.

Real-Time Quotes Bid/Ask Prices: One of the first things you'll do with your new online account is to build *watch lists.* You simply put in symbols of stocks you wish to follow and the software will give you the bid/ask prices, change for the day, the ability to pull up charts for each stock, ETF, or Index, and more.

Charting-Trading Tools: When you view charts, the horizontal axis will be time/dates and the vertical will display the prices. Begin using bar charts, which display the high, low for various (selected by you) intervals of time, like 1m, 5m,15m, 30m, 1h, 4h, 1d, 1w (minute, hour, day, week.) If you wish, you may learn more about technical indicators and charting in your software. There are a hundred or more indicators, but four or five of them are used most commonly: MACD, Bollinger Bands, Resistance-Support, Momentum, and so on. Your broker will have professionally made videos you can view free – on just about any subject.

Avoid this "beginner's mistake": It is likely better that you learn your software features "as you need them", instead of trying to learn it all before you begin. These programs are so packed with features, you would probably waste time learning many things you will never need or use. Ask your brokers suggestions on which videos best serve a beginner, and someone who will be selling covered-calls.

Statements and Trade Confirmations: Your daily transaction summary, statements, and confirmation notifications are listed in the program and usually you will receive daily email notifications of your transactions. When you enter an order, you will get a 'fill' the moment a transaction occurs – and usually a sounder to alert you also. The 'fill' is the same as a confirmation and gives you time/date stamp, transactions, prices, and other information. Paper statements are normally sent at the end of each month, but you can get your account status and balance, and a record of your transactions anytime online.

Entering Trades, Buying and Selling: Follow the instructions to enter trades, you will enter the quantity, price, and the type of order you prefer to use. (Type of orders will be explained in a section in this book.) All trading software will allow you to enter an order, and then to check it again before you SEND it; this is to avoid mistakes.

Investment Tracking: There is a section in your trading platform that will always summarize your trades, current valuation of them, and list them in an easy to interpret format. This section is sometimes called *position summary* or another similar term.

Research Educational Material: Every online broker provides customers with many tools that include charts, news items, research material, and more to help you find the information you need. Anytime you need help, you can ask your broker to suggest videos so you can train to use the software's many valuable features. It will be time well spent. You can use your smartphone or other device to watch this material on your own convenient schedule. Also, most brokers provide chat rooms where customers can talk among themselves, and this is a way to find ideas and help.

Money Transfers IN & OUT: When you open your account, you may mail a check if you wish. Most commonly, monies are transferred in/out of your account by wire transfers (or an equivalent) directly from your bank. You can call account services of your broker and they can help you set this up and answer your questions. Be aware, some banks and/or brokers charge varying rates for these services. Ask your broker for suggestions, if you need help in finding the best way for your particular needs. Often, banks have ridiculous fees to make these transfers, so be sure and ask 'how much' before you authorize the transfer.

Choosing a Broker

Online brokers typically charge from $4.95 to $12.95 per transaction (regardless of the number of shares you are trading of a stock.) To be clear: Whether you buy one share or a thousand shares, each transaction will be charged this flat fee. There is one transaction for each security (stock); you can't combine stocks into one order. Often brokers will offer a number of free trades to new accounts, so ask about that when you call.

While brokers who charge $9.95 for a trade are charging almost double the $4.95 rate, it is better to use a broker that has good software, technical service, and is a good fit for you – rather than trying to save a few dollars on stock commissions. You might save $5, but wind up with software you don't particularly like; this is not advisable. *In the long run a few dollars more in commissions here and there should not be a deal-breaker if you get the broker and the software you like.* Where you might pay $9.95 for a trade, you are still getting a good deal since full-service fees easily range from $25 and up. Most of the online brokers are charging $4.95 to $6.95 for stock trades (any number of shares); don't let trying to save two dollars keep you from getting the trading platform that is better for you.

Here's a partial list of some brokers you may wish to consider; go to their web sites and take a look at their trading platform (most will provide you samples or at least a video).

TD Ameritrade: ThinkOrSwim   Fidelity   Scott Trade (acquired by TDA)
Charles Schwab   ETrade   OptionHouse   TradeKing   Merrill EDGE

Often brokers will have more than one version of software. For example: a simple version for just buying and selling stocks; this version uses the simplest of screen interfaces and is very easy to use. Secondly, most experienced traders will opt for the version (still absolutely free) that has more features. This advanced version offers more flexibility and services. Most companies allow you to use them interchangeably – and you can switch back and forth effortlessly. Ask about this when you phone them.

The Importance of the Trade Simulation Mode

Sometimes, starting off with the more complicated trading software can be off-putting to beginners and they opt for the simpler version until they gain some confidence. Remember that your broker will have a trade simulation mode where you can learn to use the software without having to use real money. Your mistakes there won't cost you anything; this is a valuable service to learn to use the software, so go for it, explore and learn. This can be quite fun to trade paper money until you get the hang of things.

The experience of using a broker's software can vary widely, so you might wish to compare two or three before you decide. The brokers understand this; they help new customers every day. Ask questions, and see how user friendly your new broker will be!

The importance of learning to use the convenience and power of the trading software furnished to you by your broker cannot be overemphasized. Not too long ago, trading 'paper money' accounts, merely kept a list of trades and P/L (profit/loss). Now, you must learn to think of your trading software as your control center of trading and research. Being able to use your software is key to your success; it has powerful features and it will serve you well to spend the time to learn to use it. Your broker has free videos to make learning easy. Viewing several *short* videos works much better than watching hour-long videos – and this avoids information overload. As you are trading it is important to have confidence in your ability to find and use information. Use the trade simulation mode of your broker like a pilot would use a flight simulator. Think of it as a valuable and accurate trading tool and hone your skills with it so you can remain focused on your trading and not have half your attention diluted by not learning to use your software seamlessly. It's actually quite fun to trade in 'paper money' mode. It's a great way to test some ideas and gain confidence and experience without any of the risks.

Chapter 7: DRIP
Dividend Reinvestment Plans

Many stocks pay their shareholders a *dividend*, a cash payment most often paid every quarter. Dividends are a form of profit-sharing with the owners (shareholders) of the business.

Many dividend paying companies have what is called a dividend reinvestment plan (DRIP). This is a company sponsored program where shareholders may elect to have their dividends converted to more shares of the company instead of a cash payout. As the additional shares are credited to the account, those shares also will pay dividends. This is a form of *compounding* one's returns, as the shareholder who elects to have his dividend be used to buy more shares, will own more shares over time.

If you own shares in your brokerage account, you can usually sign up for a DRIP for a stock by notifying the company. Usually, this is done free of charges, and if not, there is only a small fee for setup required. Contact your broker for more information.

If you like, you can choose to contact a company directly and with the purchase of some shares, you can open a DRIP. Once you have the DRIP account directly with a company, you can buy more shares of the company commission free. You can set up plans to have a set amount deposited each month to buy more shares, or you can send them a lump sum to do so. Many companies will allow you to buy up to $250,000 of additional shares per year at no commissions. If you have multiple DRIPs, you must set up one with *each* stock, and there is no limit to how many you may have.

I hasten to add that opening these accounts is as easy as signing up to have your utilities turned on. Sometimes, there is a one-time charge to set up a DRIP; it is a relatively small fee and you are required to buy at least one share of the stock.

Let's examine a common stock and it's DRIP. McDonalds (symbol MCD) is owned by millions of people and it trades millions of shares every day. To illustrate how much a DRIP can increase your returns over time, here is an example.

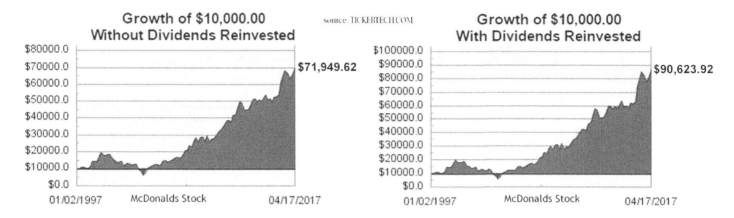

These two charts display MCD stock Without Dividends Reinvested versus With Dividends Reinvested in a little over 20 years. The yield with dividends reinvested is 25.9% more!

Just think how much better you can do if you take full advantage of Covered CALL writing and the DRIP. Plus you still get regular capitals gains from your stocks. This is truly "triple income" results.

Also note in the chart comparisons, the original investment of $10,000 did NOT include any additional deposits/contributions.

Consider Your Choices

Stock Split

Since going public in 1965, McDonald's has executed twelve stock splits. In fact, an investment of $2,250 in 100 shares at that time has grown to 74,360 shares worth approximately $9.1 million as of market close on December 30, 2016.

McDonald's Stock Split History

	Type	Record Date	Distribution Date
1.	2 for 1	Feb 12, 1999	Mar 5, 1999
2.	2 for 1	Jun 7, 1994	Jun 24, 1994
3.	2 for 1	Jun 2, 1989	Jun 16, 1989
4.	3 for 2	Jun 8, 1987	Jun 22, 1987
5.	3 for 2	Jun 3, 1986	Jun 25, 1986
6.	3 for 2	Sep 5, 1984	Sep 24, 1984
7.	3 for 2	Sep 14, 1982	Oct 6, 1982
8.	2 for 1	May 22, 1972	Jun 5, 1972
9.	3 for 2	May 21, 1971	Jun 11, 1971
10.	2 for 1	May 23, 1969	Jun 13, 1969
11.	2 for 1	May 7, 1968	May 20, 1968
12.	2% Stock Dividend	Mar 20, 1967	Apr 10, 1967
13.	3 for 2	Mar 29, 1966	Apr 18, 1966

A STOCK SPLIT is when a company issues additional shares to shareholders based on how many shares they hold. There is no gain or loss, as the new shares are assigned on a weighted basis reflecting the share price. Example: If a $50 stock splits 2 for 1, the shareholder gets two shares valued at $25 each.

STOCK TOTAL RETURN CALCULATOR

Stock Ticker: MCD   **Starting Amount ($):**   10000

Starting Date: 04/20/1996   **Ending Date:**   04/16/2016

Calculate   Reset

ADVANCED OPTIONS

- Only touch these if you want to model adding money to the account periodically.
- By default, only dividends will be reinvested.

Reinvestment ($):   100   **Frequency:**   Every 4th Week ▼

RESULTS

Total Amount : $139,046.41   **Annualized Return:**   9.70%

source of table: https://dqydj.com/stock-return-calculator-dividend-reinvestment-drip/

Here the actual results of 20 years April 1996 to April 2016 for MCD stock with dividends and stock splits applied. NOTE: In the example, the initial investment is $10,000 with an additional $100 added every 4 weeks.

A wonderful thing about DRIP, anyone who wants to gift a minor child stock can buy only 1 or more shares to open an account for the child. This is called a Uniform Gift to Minors Act (UGMA) account. It's a great started account to help teach children about investing.

You can do a one time account setup and stock-buy.

You can setup periodic contributions to buy stock (no commissions).

You may (in most of these DRIPs) buy up to $250,000 of additional stock at no commission charge.

You can redeem (sell your shares and get a check sent) at any time.

How To Open a DRIP

The instructions are very simple:

1) Google the stock company name and shareholder services. For example: "McDonalds shareholder services".
2) There is a one or two page application and all it requires is name, address, the social security number of the adult or (custodial account) child's social security.
3) Most companies only require you buy one share. Some have minimum amounts of a few hundred dollars. Most account setup fees are either free or a charge from $5 to $50, they vary.

Please keep in mind these companies have offices who help people open these accounts by the dozens everyday. So phone or look them up on the web and ask all the questions you like. If you'd like to see a typical shareholder services website, see: http://corporate.mcdonalds.com/mcd/investors/shareholder-information/investor_tools/how_to_buy_stock.html

I have selected McDonalds (MCD) for the example in this section, only because it is an example of a household name, large cap, widely traded, stock. The examples used in this book are not intended to be investment advice. If you would like to receive the free BONUS Chapter for this book, it has more examples and links to websites that can be helpful as you learn more about covered calls, DRIPs, and stock & option selection.

To get the free BONUS chapter, just send me an email at Don@WriteThisDown.com and put COVERED CALL in the subject line. This free information contains tips for dividend stock selection, selecting good candidates for covered-call selling, and stocks with DRIPs. If you have a question or comment, just drop me an email; I'd be glad to hear from you.

Chapter 8: Purposes of Stock Option Trading

Options for Income

The surest, safest way to make option income money is to sell options. The primary strategy is writing (selling) covered-CALL options. Selling options on stocks you already own (or will buy) is a strategy so safe it is approved for use in self-directed retirement accounts.   This strategy can easily add 5 to 15% or more to the returns on your account, and the strategy works in bull, bear, and neutral markets. In many cases, depending on how your money is invested, it can actually double the return on your retirement funds. Most people don't know about it, hesitate to learn more – and so are missing out on one of the greatest boons to personal investments of a lifetime. Once you learn this strategy and gain a little experience, it might only take an hour or two a month for you to significantly add earnings power in your retirement account. *Selling options on your long-term buy and hold stocks can be the safest application of option trading that is available and also one of the most common and easiest.* This type of trading is considered smart and passive. Many fund managers use it all the time to increase performance in stock funds. If you own stocks, this is a great way to get your feet wet and gain some experience without significant risk exposure. Just to be clear, when I say "safe", this requires a conditional note: When Covered CALL writing is used on stocks you either will buy, or already own, writing the call does not add additional risk, *you always have the risk of a stock's price going down.* Covered CALL selling does not add *additional* risk.

Sophisticated option strategies are available for all risk tolerance levels. One of the most valuable lessons you will learn about trading options is that they have a 'risk control' that is not unlike the volume control on a radio or TV; you can select from a range of risks and possible rewards.   You not only select a strategy (type of trade), you also choose the risk level by choosing which *strikes* to use, and which stocks and market views to employ (tactical). For professional option traders, *option spreads* – not outright buying of PUTS and CALLS- are preferred trades and there is a reason for this: They are the trades that give you the most control of risk in trade selections.

Vertical Spreads with options describe the most commonly used combination strategies by beginners and advanced traders. Investors who own stocks in trading and tax-deferred accounts will want to consider the covered call strategies, collars, and also techniques of rolling out covered options to increase return on equity in these accounts.

Protection and Hedges

In building financial wealth and security, making profits trading is only half of the task; the other equally important half is learning to keep the money you make. Wealthy investors actively use risk management techniques to protect investments, while surprisingly few individual investors with self-directed accounts are aware of these relatively inexpensive and easy strategies to protect the gains they have made. No one questions the necessity and wisdom of insuring their car, home, and life – but we are not commonly taught how to do the same by strategizing protection in our retirement accounts. Traditionally, financial advisors advise almost everyone to use what is called *asset allocation*; that is dividing your investments between categories like: stocks, bonds, real estate, precious metals, and other strategies. What often happens is that most investors have most of their funds in stocks, and when the market crashes and/or particular stocks fail, a great deal of hard-earned profits are lost. Many financial planners allow investors - and even condition them - to expect large losses as an inevitable part of their stock portfolio – and they are not totally wrong. What you may not know - is that sophisticated and wealthier investors will not tolerate that advice; when they have large gains - they understand the good practices of protecting their gains. The regular everyday well-meaning investors are also trained by many money managers and financial advisors to diversify, so 'when the market varies you won't have all your eggs in one basket'. "Spread the risks," they say - among dozens of stocks. In other words, if you buy stocks or other investments, adapt a passive attitude and learn to take your lumps and do nothing. You should seriously question this attitude.

There is a very popular investor who has ignored this advice for years and is one of the richest people in the world, Warren Buffett. There are some good books on how he does it and well-worth the read, but I am going to share, in my own words of course, what I believe to be the essence of this genius investor. What I admire most about Warren Buffett is that what he does is little more than common sense and quite logical, and yet it goes against virtually every money manager that urges people to diversify widely to avoid risks. I'll explain it right now in simple language and you make up your own mind: If you owned a stable of 100 thoroughbred race horses, and 10% of them won 95% of the races, why would you enter all 100 or even 80 of them in the races? You wouldn't! And that, my friend, is how easy it is to show you the essence of good investing. There is a current day movement among modern managers that is ditching the long-held -and perhaps overly simplistic view- of safety in diversification – and it's about time. This doesn't negate nor deny investing in various *kinds* of assets for safety, but if you are going to put money in stocks, you might want ten good ones instead of buying 100 with a shotgun approach. And when you do get those windfall profits, you might consider protecting profits instead of just passively letting it ride – as a strategy.

Learning to use options for protection is nothing more than choosing the right tool for the right job. It makes perfect sense to learn to make better choices about protecting what you have made. You took risks to make that money and it paid off; now *doing nothing* to protect it may be taking risk unnecessarily. Savvy investors know that *doing nothing* is a choice with consequences. If you made 50% profits in your account in five years, would you spend 1% of your profits to protect it? You probably answered 'yes'; options can be an inexpensive way to protect what you've already accomplished – and in the long run, keeping what you make will have you making even more. Anyone who learns to make money but fails to learn how to keep it, doesn't really understand investing; they only have half of the equation. A stock with a high beta tracks the larger market, perhaps mirroring the S&P 500 or another index; options on an index can be used to hedge profits. Have you ever plotted your retirement fund's performance against an index like the S&P 500? That's what one does to see if options on that index are a viable way of hedging your profits against downside sliding.

Using options on ETF's -*exchange traded funds* – that track major indexes like the DJIA or S&P500 is a great way to use options to protect you from poor stock market performance. Understand also, that this protection is not just an 'on-off' function but can be used to hedge to various degrees. It isn't just an all or nothing proposition. There are ETF's available for very specific market segments too, like petroleum, interest rates, or pharmaceuticals. Not all ETF's have options available.

Speculation

One of the major advantages available to option traders is *leverage*. Buying 100 shares of a $125 stock would cost $12,500 while buying the CALL option might be close to $800. In effect, you are controlling a large value of the stock for a relatively small amount of money. The stock shares are a risk in value equal to the purchase price, while the option maximum loss is the cost of the option only. Unlike buying the stock, the option purchase has an expiration date, so timing is a major consideration when using options instead of buying the underlying stock. And there are ways to use option spreads to reduce both the cost and the risks of speculative trades. You can just as easily find option strategies for bull, bear, or neutral plays. Clearly, buying options is a speculative venture. When you buy options, you pay a price that most times, already has the "market expectations" price-in, and this makes this practice more risky.

The Attractions of Option Trading

The leverage: Controlling large assets with a small amount of money.
Flexibility: Being able to make money in any type of market – bull, bear, neutral
Risk Selection: Be in control of the amount of risk you take on any investment play.
Protection: Having economical ways of protecting money you have already made.

All of the above are great - but the thing I enjoy most about option trading is that I can open my office anywhere I can get an internet connection. My second favorite thing about trading options is the strategy of *selling* them. About 80% of options expire worthless; this means the odds are in my favor from the very start of these trades. As you read more about how this works, you will realize you can make money selling options even when your market view is wrong. You will learn how to use your online trading platform to measure the risk of each of these trades and to calculate the probability of profit of each and every trade. I didn't say it was easy and I didn't say you will always make money, but the smarter you learn to trade – the luckier you'll get!

I think a great many online traders of stocks, options, commodities, and other products – all share the fantasy of sitting under a palm tree at the beach being able to use our computer/mobile device - to make money. The idea of using our own resources and wits to pursue profits from just about any location at any time, is something that appeals to most women and men. Truth be told, I don't really need the beach and palm tree so much; I just enjoy the freedom and sense of achievement. And I have to say, being able to have the resources, the time, the opportunity - and the freedom and good health to do all this - is something I never take for granted. The third thing I love most about option trading is being able to share what I know with people and making new friends with like-minded people.

One common myth about trading options is that there are only a few types of traders. In fact, options offer so many choices, that you will eventually find the strategies and risk tolerance that will be a fit for you. We all have different tastes for food and our preferences in types of music – and you will also find what suits you best as you gain experience with options. There are plenty of strategies for very conservative types and for all speculators.

Time Value & Theta

Theta is a function of premium time-decay; the higher the theta, the faster the option's premium decreases. Theta is represented in an actual dollar or premium amount and is usually calculated and display as the value for the current trading day. Theta represents, in theory, how much an option's premium may decay per day with all other things remaining the same.

Example: XYZ stock is trading at 80, the XYZ DEC 90 CALL trades at 2.35 and has a theta of .05 This option can be expected to lose .05 off its premium in a day due to time decay.   If you are short 10 of these CALLS and theta is .05, then – all other things being the same – you can expect the value of the ten options to decrease by (.05 x 10) $50 a day.

If you are buying an option, you might shop options with a low theta, and conversely – if you are selling an option a higher theta would indicate a faster rate of premium decay. Time decay is not linear: During the life of an option, the rate of its time decay increases as it is nearer to expiration, so it's theta might increase (all other things equal), but as the option is very close (a few days perhaps), the theta can decrease because the value of the options extrinsic value is nearing zero. Remember theta is not the rate of time decay but the amount. Extrinsic value is the portion of the premium not caused by being ITM (IV% value and time value).

The slope on the time-decay graph indicates a faster drop off of time value in the last 30 days of an option's life. Since theta is the daily amount the premium atrophies due to time-decay, the value of theta generally goes up as the option nears expiration. This is precisely why option sellers wishing to collect premium from time-decay prefer shorter term options (fewer days until expiration, or the 'nearby' class of an underlying's options – sometimes called the *front month*). This does not negate the importance of a having a market bias or viewpoint when selling options, but many times when the underlying's price may go up and down, the time-decay is still on-going.

There are two good reasons the seller of an option prefers to short far OTM options:
1) There is less probability the option will expire ITM or be called away (higher Prob OTM% than ATM, ITM, and nearby strikes).
2) Almost all of the option's premium value is time value (the other major component is IV%).

note: all the terms and explanations to begin option trading to use sophisticated strategies are in *Options Exposed Playbook.*

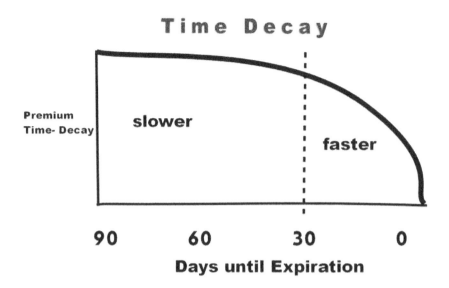

Other books by the author

Every reader deserves to be lead straight to point without excessive pep talks, and chatter of making easy money. It is my belief that far too many writers, financial reporters, and money advisors try to rise themselves by making simple things complicated. I just published a book with this subtitle: **The Easiest Guide to Personal Investing Ever Written**

It is a book that a person who knows little-to-nothing about the stock market, can spend less than two hours with - and they will have the knowledge and understanding to confidently invest in stocks. It's a book with a lot of common-sense from well-known investment masters, time-tested, illustrated, simple and proven methods - that are common-sense and almost no math. It's the type of book that a lot of people have needed for a long time. I get emails from parents that have bought copies for their sons, daughters, and grandkids.

Only about three stock investors of a every hundred understand and use option trading, even though they are a top investment tool.   *Options Exposed Playbook* is a solid introduction to trading options and has over 20 top strategies illustrated. This book has been used by thousands of option traders and has become know for its easy-to-read and plain language introduction to options.

Thank you for your support.

Made in the USA
Monee, IL
10 February 2021